The Fundamentals of Money and Financial Systems

The Fundamentals of Money and Financial Systems

Shahdad Naghshpour

business**expert**
Press

HUMBER LIBRARIES LAKESHORE CAMPUS
3199 Lakeshore Blvd West
TORONTO, ON.   M8V 1K8

First published in 2013 by
Business Expert Press, LLC
222 East 46th Street, New York, NY 10017
www.businessexpertpress.com

ISBN-13: 978-1-60649-484-4 (paperback)
ISBN-13: 978-1-60649-485-1 (e-book)

Business Expert Press Economics collection

Collection ISSN: 2163-761X (print)
Collection ISSN: 2163-7628 (electronic)

Cover and interior design by Exeter Premedia Services Private Ltd.,
Chennai, India

First edition: 2013

10 9 8 7 6 5 4 3 2 1

Printed in the United States of America.

To Kaylie
SN

Abstract

It is impossible to comprehend what policies the government should undertake to face the economic reality of the country. Every day the public is exposed to a barrage of recommendations and mandates from the left and the right concerning what would be the appropriate course of action or lack thereof in order to nullify economic ills or to bring prosperity to the country. A fundamentally basic requirement to being able to comprehend these claims is the knowledge of money.

It is important to understand the meaning of money and be able to differentiate between basic concepts such as consumption, savings, capital, and investment. Would it make any difference, to the overall function of the economy, earnings, employment, etc. if a given sum of money is spent by an individual, a small business, a corporation, or the government? Is it good for the country if people spend money or is it better if they save it? Would it make a difference if spending originates from printing money or citizens' savings? The answer to these and many other economic questions are at the heart of the fiscal and monetary policy that every government grapples with every day. It is essential to know the role of money and how it fits into the answers to these and other policy questions.

This book provides the necessary foundations for understanding money and many of its functions, roles, and uses in economic theories that are essential to comprehend economic theories needed for formulation of fiscal and monetary policies. This book is not a textbook to be used in a course in money and banking in a typical economic program. It is written for executives and decision makers who need to comprehend the meanings of different policies and how they affect their decisions in their business or private life but cannot even begin the process because they are unaware of the basic block of fiscal and monetary policy, namely money. Many people use the words like capital, savings, and investments interchangeably or as close substitutes. However, each one has a specific meaning and purpose in economics. After reading this book you will be ready to understand the fiscal and monetary policies, tools, and effectiveness.

Keywords

bank, banking, capital, consumption, Federal Reserve, liquidity, monetary, money, savings, transaction, speculative, quantity theory.

Contents

List of Symbols

The numbers in parentheses refer to the chapters in which the symbol is used.

A	Autonomous Spending (11)
AD	Aggregate Demand (11)
b	Responsiveness of Investment to the Interest Rate (11)
c	Transaction Cost (2)
C	Consumption (11)
C_0	Subsistence Level of consumption (11)
D	Discounted Present Value (9)
E	Expected Value (9)
G	Government Expenditure (11)
i	Interest Rate (2, 3, 4, 5, 7, 8, 9, 11, 12)
i_b	Rate of Return on Bonds (4)
i_e	Rate of Return on Equities (4)
i_m	Rate of Return on Money (4)
iP	Opportunity Cost of Receiving Funds in One Year (8)
I	Investment (11)
k	Average length of holding money of Money (1, 2)
m	Responsiveness of Demand for Money to Income (12)
$M1$	Narrow definition of Money (Introduction, 4, 6)
$M2$	Broader and less liquid definition of money (Introduction, 4, 6)
$M3$	Broader and less liquid definition of money that includes M2 plus time deposits at mutual savings banks and savings and loan associations, and shares held at credit unions (Introduction, 6)
$M4$	Broader and less liquid definition of money that includes M2 plus negotiable CDs over \$100,000 (Introduction, 6)
$M5$	Broader and less liquid definition of money that includes M3 plus negotiable CDs over \$100,000 (Introduction, 6)
M^d	Demand for Money (1, 2, 12)
MPC	Marginal Propensity to Consume (11)
MPS	Marginal Propensity to Save (11)
n	Responsiveness of Demand for Money to Interest Rate (12)

Acknowledgments

I am indebted to my wife Donna who has helped me in more ways than imaginable. I do not think I can thank her enough. I would like to thank Candace Bright, Brian Carriere, David Davis, Charles Tibedo, and Michael Webb, all doctoral students at the International Development and International Affairs of the University of Southern Mississippi. They have provided many hours of help with all aspects of the process. Without the help of Brian, Candace, Charles, Dave, and Mike the book would not have been completed. They have provided valuable suggestions to improve the quality. Any remaining shortcomings rest solely on my shoulders.

Introduction

According to some historians, money has been used for at least 3,200 years, in one form or another. Throughout most of this period, it was very difficult to think of an economy without money. However, with the advent of online banking and direct payment, most people no longer see their "money," although they still have income and conduct transactions. The concern here is not about pinpointing the exact day that money was invented, or in giving an account of all the different, and at times exotic things that have been used as money in different parts of the world. Rather, the focus is on the conditions that give rise to the exchange of goods and services. For this reason, the concept of an economy without money in the form of hard currency is much easier to comprehend for someone in the twenty-first century than it was in previous centuries.

Barter

Some believe there was a time before the invention of money when people bartered. **Barter** is the exchange of one thing for another, when neither good is "money." This definition implies that if one is "paid" for work using goods other than money, the transaction is considered to be barter. The implication is that not only production for the purpose of trade precedes the creation of money but also that either the production exceeded consumption or that division of labor and expertise had occurred before the notion of money was realized. They also imply highly developed societies that have a concept of individual ownership, which was neither common nor universal in human history. The notion of working for pay or receiving payments for property is foreign to communal and tribal ways of life, which still exist in some areas. The means of production, such as land, equipment, and capital, have traditionally been owned communally in such tribes. Communal ownership of property is not limited to primitive underdeveloped areas. For example, in 2011, the community of Saranac Lake, New York, decided to communally own the town's department store.

The concept of barter, or more generally, the notion of exchange, requires one person to have more of an item than s/he needs and at the same time someone else to have a similar dilemma with another good. In order to have a need for any exchange, via barter or money, it is necessary to have private ownership. Furthermore, the good that one person is willing to give up must be exactly the same as the good the other person is willing to obtain. In light of all the problems that plague bartering, I am not sure that bartering was as common as some would argue, or that it predated money transactions. **Money** is any medium that is acceptable by the public to serve the *purposes* of money.

So far, we have identified two prerequisites for any exchange, regardless of whether it is through barter or via money exchange. First, there must be private ownership, and second, there must be an excess supply of a good. It is not rational to produce more of a good than one can consume, unless one knows that he can exchange it for something else. However, if one needs something else, the logical action is to obtain it directly. For the purpose of demonstration; focus on the time period when humans were gatherers. If a person was hungry, he would eat the first thing that was edible, say figs. He would consume figs until the **marginal utility** of figs became equal to the **marginal cost** of figs. In economics, the word "marginal" refers to the last unit of the phenomenon under consideration. Thus, the marginal utility is the utility derived from consumption of the last unit of fig. The first fig of the day is more valuable than the last one. A hungry man would be willing to exert more effort, i.e. endure greater cost, to find the first fig of the day as compared to the last fig, when he is almost satisfied. Thus, the utility of figs, as any other good, declines as more of it is consumed per unit of time. On the other hand, the cost of producing, i.e. searching and finding, figs increases. Logically, one would pick the "low-hanging" fruits first before climbing to the top of the tree. As the low-hanging fruits disappear the cost of picking figs increases. When the utility from consumption of one more fig becomes less than the cost of producing it the search will end. For this example, the marginal cost of picking figs is the effort exerted to pick them from the tree, which is almost zero. Although he may be hungry again during the same day, he might not have much utility for eating figs after having had enough figs for lunch.

It is illogical to collect more figs than one can eat unless there is assurance that there is another individual with a different product for exchange for figs. Therefore, the knowledge that someone else has an excess of another desirable commodity is necessary before one gathers more figs than he can consume. In the event that there is no trade possibility, the marginal utility of excess figs is zero for our gatherer. This discussion does not preclude the existence of responsibility for caring for family members and friends or charity. A person might pick more figs than he can consume in order to feed his family, share with a friend, or to be charitable. Nevertheless, we can easily consider the combined amount as one's consumption in the previous analysis.

Similar dilemmas afflict other producers/gatherers. Suppose a second individual has picked apples and after consuming enough his marginal utility for apples is zero for the day, but he picks extra apples hoping to be able to trade them. The two traders will be glad to get something for their commodities, as their own commodities have zero marginal utility for them. Therefore, in this simplistic situation the first person should be willing to give all his excess figs to receive all the excess apples. This demonstrates the first problem of bartering. The value of the excess commodity is zero for its owner, but positive for other people. If there are others with tradable goods, the man with figs should be able to exchange his fig for the commodity that gives him the most utility. Let us suppose that the commodity is almonds. However, for the sake of demonstration, let us assume that the person with almonds does not wish to have figs, but he would like to have apples. In order for the first person to obtain almonds he must first exchange the figs for apples, and then exchange the apples for almonds. This process increases the cost of transaction, because it may be necessary to have several transactions instead of one to finally obtain the good from which an individual gains the most utility. Since each transaction adds to cost, transactions reduce the utility.

Under this scenario, we immediately end up with a "professional trader" who does nothing but trade one good for another, otherwise known as a merchant. This is inevitable if there is any utility in exchanging one good for another anytime a perfect match is lacking. However, this requires the ability to obtain goods beyond what one can consume per period. The existence of a merchant to facilitate trade of excess of production over consumption provides another reason for invention of money. The merchant would choose goods that are easily convertible to other goods. In other words, he would prefer a "liquid" commodity. Money satisfies this function. Money is **liquid** in the sense that it can be used to obtain other goods without requiring additional transactions.

Problems of Barter

In the above process, we introduced another problem of bartering, namely the problem of exact matching of bartered goods. Imagine the frustration of picking watermelons and taking them to the market to find out that they are not in demand. To make matters worse, imagine you find someone who wants some watermelons, but has another product, such as cantaloupes, that you do not want, but might be able to exchange them with someone else who has a commodity that is more desirable to you. Notice that we are deliberately choosing perishable items to highlight the problem. Non-perishable items postpone the inevitable problem demonstrated in this example.

There are other problems with bartering. One of these is the inability to find the exact market value of the goods. How many figs should be exchanged for how many apples? Note that in the first example above, both parties would be glad to give all their figs and apples to each other because the marginal utility for their own product is zero, provided there are no other traders. In the presence of other goods and traders, the amount of computation becomes staggering but the original dilemma remains the same. All the traders must know the exact ratio for all the goods and services available for exchange for any given day. Hidden in the above cases is the problem that goods must be divisible. For example, if the item for exchange is lumber, a non- perishable good, it must be sold as a unit to be useful. Lumber that is cut up into small pieces cannot be used in construction in the same way a large piece could be used. A long piece of lumber will require lots of figs for a fair exchange. As another example, suppose you have enough figs for only half of a piece of lumber, or suppose that in the market, three watermelons would exchange for five chickens, but you only have two watermelons and the other person has only three chickens. To make matters worse, you only need one chicken, and the other person needs one and a half melons. Any time that a good loses its value over time, such as perishable goods, it cannot store **value**. Money is more dependable for storing value. Finally, money is able to store **wealth.** In a barter system with no commonly accepted money, the wealth cannot be stored. Note that the specific type of money that is used for storing wealth does not matter as long as it is accepted for that purpose. For example, in Massai culture, cattle is used as a store of wealth, thus, it is a form of money. In summary, we can list the following problems as arising from the barter system:

Requires double-coincidence of wants

Requires goods that are divisible

Requires the knowledge of market value for many goods

Cannot store value easily

Cannot store wealth easily

This list, however, is not exhaustive, as one can identify additional problems that can arise in typical transactions.

The majority of the problems of barter are simply inconveniences, because they can be resolved rather easily by using money. In fact, every human community has "invented" money or utilized the concept. Soon we will see the advantages of money, which overcome the problems associated with barter and then some. Because of the problems with barter it is doubtful that humanity traded through barter before using money. The exception being when needs and goods were easily matched. I do not mean to imply that no one ever worked for someone else in return for a good other than money or traded using barter; this conduct still occurs today. Anytime you perform a favor for a friend and he or she reciprocates the favor you have engaged in barter. The advent of the Internet has sparked a new era of barter. In today's economy barter is another way of conducting transactions, instead of serving as a replacement for money. Many countries actually trade on the basis of barter. In fact, in international trade, no money actually changes hand. The accounts of countries are debited and credited on the basis of purchases or sales. The books are balanced at the end of the year, but even then, no money changes hand, except in rare occasions, such as when the political relationship between two countries sours. In general, the balance at the end of the year is carried to the next year as an entry in the balance of payment books. An important exception was during the balance of trade deficit of the mid 1960s when France under the presidency of General de Gaulle in 1965 demanded gold bullion from the United States in return for its accumulated dollars under a deliberate process to acquire and hold dollar. The move was in response to the fact that the price of gold was being kept artificially low by maintaining an overvalued dollar to finance the War in Vietnam through balance of payment deficit. Over time, maintaining the price of gold at the official rate of $35 per ounce became more difficult. Finally, in 1971 President Nixon led the effort to end the gold standard, and thus, completely fiat money was established around the world. **Fiat money** is a currency without precious metal backing. The value of fiat money stems from the dependability of the government that issues it.

The Myth of the Intrinsic Value of Money

One of the main objections to fiat money was the idea that money has to have an intrinsic value in order to buy other things. However, any item that is accepted by transacting parties can be used as money. Money is used to buy a good, whose value is stored in the money, then that value is converted to another good later. According to Friedman (1965), money is the temporary abode of purchasing power. As such, any agreed upon object would serve the purpose. Therefore, the myth that money must have an intrinsic value is not valid. Money is any object that the society accepts. Some of the commodities that have been used as money are seemingly worthless, in the sense that they lack intrinsic value, at least in today's economy. To be practical, an item that is used as money must have the following properties:

Useful
Durable
Commonly known and available
Require little or no additional cost

Portable

Reliable

Dependable

Hard to falsify

Numerous objects such as salt, livestock, cowry shells, beads, precious stones, precious metals, paper, and plastic have all, at one time and place or another, been used as money. The list is not meant to be exhaustive, but rather informative. As is evident, certain items used as money meet some of the above criteria better than others. Overtime, the choices of items for money have evolved to their present day form of paper money and plastic. The advent of computer technology and methods of electronic identification may soon eliminate the need for currency in the familiar form. All items that have ever been used as money have a production cost. Some of the items used as money had intrinsic value as well, but that is not the case for the most recent forms of money, namely plastic cards and paper money without precious stones or metal backing. Compared to their face values, modern money is very inexpensive to produce. However, if we think carefully, we realize that some items, such as cowry shells, can only have value as ornaments, and for most of history the coins of precious metals had less precious metal in them than the face value of the coin. These facts cast doubt on the necessity of an intrinsic value for the money.

Economists are more interested in different aspects of money than the historical accounts addressed above. Economists are interested why people want money. Of course economists examine this question from the economics perspective. The demand for money is addressed in Section I of this book. Section II consists of two chapters and is devoted to the supply of money, focusing on The Federal Reserve and commercial banks as the suppliers of money. Section III clarifies the role of interest rate in the demand for and the supply of money. Section IV discusses the components of the financial systems and the equilibrium of goods and money markets in separate chapters. Chapter 13 provides a conclusion and a brief discussion of monetary and fiscal policies.

It is important to provide a definition for money. However, as will become evident in Section II, the concept of money is so closely related to the notion of supply of money, that it is almost impossible to define money without inadvertently explaining the supply of money. Customarily, the definition of things explains what they are completely, but we will have to wait until Section II to accomplish this task in the case of money. Consequently, we will define the term here broadly.

Definition

Money is anything that is customarily accepted by parties engaged in a transaction or financial arrangement. The word "customarily" in the definition excludes barter.

Properties of Money

Money serves, or should serve, several purposes, such as a medium of exchange, a unit of account, and a store of value.

Medium of Exchange

One problem with barter is the necessity for a double-coincidence of wants. By introducing money into transactions, this problem is solved. You sell your surplus of goods and services and obtain money, then use money to purchase what you are lacking.

Unit of Account

Another problem with barter is the inability, or at least the difficulty, to determine the exchange rate of different goods and services in terms of each other. Even when an individual's surplus equals the shortage of another person, it is not easy to find out the rate of exchange for the two goods in the market. Money facilitates exchange, because it converts the price of each item into units of money instead.

Store of Value

Another useful function of money is the ability to extend the value of goods and services to future periods, possibly to future generations, in the form of bequest. Converting goods and services eliminates loss due to spoilage of goods. It also stores the value of human effort. Think of a gatherer in ancient times who collected enough food for his family for the day—there would be no point in working any more since excess food will spoil by the next day. However, if he could convert the excess food into money, then the money could store the value until needed. The use of money preserves a precious good, maybe the most precious good, namely human time. Time not used in production is lost forever. However, converting the value of labor into money stores its value for future consumption.

These properties of money indicate that money might be valuable in and of itself, which means it might be treated like any other good or service. Like any other economic good, money is scarce, and hence, it can be of value. In today's economy, in order to obtain money, we either have to work or sell accumulated labor in the form of goods. In the past, when other types of goods were used for money, people could either work for the money, as is customary presently, or collect the money themselves. For example, when cowry shells were used as money, people could collect money from its source. The same is true about other kinds of money, such as gold but not true of fiat money.

Even when people could pick up cowry shells or dig up gold, the nature of money was not different than present day money. In all cases, money is scarce, like any other economic good. Consequently, when studying money, we take advantage of existing economic theories that are applicable.

Ironically, when comparing money to other means of storing value, it is not necessarily the best way to store value over time. For instance, instead of storing the value of excess production over current consumption in the form of money, money can be lent to those whose present consumption exceeds their current production. Lending money involves parting with something valuable, not enjoying things you could be consuming, and accepting the risk of losing it. The interest received is a compensation for risk, therefore, the **interest rate** is the **price of money**.

Money in the Modern Economy

It seems anything could be considered as money, so long as it possesses the properties of being a medium of exchange, unit of account, and store of value. Obviously, the currency of a country, in the form of coins and paper bills, is considered money. In addition, when the currency is placed in a checking account it is still money and almost as liquid as the currency. Therefore, the sum of all the checking accounts in the country is part of the supply of money. The nomenclature for a checking account is **demand deposit**, while that of savings account is **time deposit**. The reason is that for a while, money that was placed in a savings account could not be withdrawn upon demand and there was a waiting period, while the money in a checking account had to be paid upon demand. Therefore, the demand deposit is more liquid than the savings deposit. The terminology stems from the fact that by law, banking institutions can require up to thirty days before paying money deposited in a savings account. However, since the last quarter of the twentieth century, banks have not exercised this right. The fact that money is less liquid by virtue of being in a savings account does not make it less of money. Based on the **liquidity,** money is classified into types called M1, M2, M3, M4, or M5, which will be discussed in detail in Chapter 6. The most liquid form of money is anything that is accepted as medium of exchange. This excludes some of the forms of money that are better at storing value.

SECTION I

Demand for Money

CHAPTER 1

The Quantity Theory

Demand for Money

Economists view money like any other good or service, with one exception: money does not provide a direct utility, whereas most other goods do. We enjoy eating chocolates, taking a drive, going on a vacation, and so forth. There are numerous other things in life that do not have direct utility. For example, a television set does not have a direct utility by itself, as it is useless without a television program. We demand television sets because television programs have direct utility. Most durable equipment, such as washing machines, automobiles, and printers, provide indirect utilities; they are valued for the services they provide. One can split hairs and claim that some people might like a car for what it is, get utility from a refrigerator, or love money for the sake of money; however, we are not interested in such semantic discussions. There are many goods, including money, that are demanded because they provide indirect utility. Although money does not have direct utility, it is demanded because it can be readily used to buy other goods that provide either direct or indirect utility.

Viewing money as one of many goods and services has advantages and disadvantages. Treating money like other goods allows us to use the same economic laws and theories applicable to other goods. The first set of laws that applies to money is the laws of supply and demand. Understanding these laws is essential for understanding the more complex issues of fiscal and monetary theories. This book is devoted to explaining the concept of money and financial institutions with a focus on supply and demand for money. This prepares you for understanding fiscal policy[1] and monetary policy.[2]

Over time, different views have evolved that address and explain the demand for money. The *quantity theory*, which will be covered in this chapter, provides the oldest explanation for demand for money in modern economics. This theory has become the foundation of monetary policy.[2] Chapter 2 discusses the *transaction theory's* explanation of demand for money. Later, you will see that the foundations of *fiscal policy* were formed by economists who only viewed the transaction theory of money as important and overlooked the classical monetary theory. This topic is the focus of fiscal policy discussion.[1] Chapter 3 provides an explanation for demand for money called *portfolio balances*. Finally, Chapter 4 wraps up the demand-for-money discussion by addressing modern theories and providing a brief discussion on estimating the demand for money.

The Quantity Theory

Although the quantity theory of money dates back to the age of Cantillon and Hume in the eighteenth century, Irving Fisher of the twentieth century is usually given the credit for the concept. Fisher's approach, which is often referred to as the transaction approach to the quantity theory of money, defines the demand for money from a macroeconomics perspective. The model ascertains that the demand for money is a multiple of the total money expenditures (price times output), which in turn is the nominal gross domestic product (GDP). The *equation of exchange* is given as follows:[3]

$$MV = PQ \qquad (1.1)$$

where V is the velocity of money (M), which is assumed to be fairly stable over time for a given economy, P is the price level, and Q is the output of the economy, at least in a closed economy.[3]

Definition

The *velocity* of money represents the average number of times money changes hand in a year.

A closed economy is one that does not engage in foreign trade. There are few countries without trade. There have been periods of restricted trade in some countries, by choice or by force as in embargo. The United States, for example, went through a period of isolationism in the early nineteenth century. Assuming an economy is closed simplifies the discussion without considering any of the prevailing relationships. Both Cantillon and Hume, when addressing the mercantilism doctrine, use this concept and relationship in their discussion.[4] The relationship in equation 1.1 expresses the demand for money at the national level as a function of prices, national income, and the inverse of the velocity of money. The product "PQ" represents the nominal income of the country, which is defined as the sum of the values of all the income generated in the country. Although the concept is easily understood, obtaining the national income by multiplying the output by price is almost impossible because different products have different prices. To obtain national income from the outputs of goods and services and their prices, multiply each good by its price and add them up. In practice, the total market value of all the goods and services that were produced and purchased in the country is used. The velocity of money is another variable that conceptually is easy to comprehend, but it is difficult to measure.

The amount of money in circulation is the same whether a one-hundred dollar bill changes hands five times or five one-hundred dollar bills are exchanged in the course of a year. In the case of the former, the velocity is five times faster than in the case of the latter. Of course, there is no way of knowing how many times each piece of money changes hands during the course of the year, although there are statistical procedures to estimate the velocity.[3] Moreover, except when the physical amount of money in circulation is equal to the national income, each unit of currency must change hands several times in order to pay for all the transactions. Therefore, to obtain the velocity of money, add the value of all the country's transactions in one year, and then divide it by the available currency. Empirically, we can regress total income on the supply of money.[5] Alternatively, we can also use the value of output, such as GDP instead of income.[6]

According to Fisher, the velocity of money depends on a country's financial institutions.[3] These institutions have procedural and habitual ways of performing transactions. For example, in the twenty-first century, many people shop online, use their credit cards for payment, or make direct transfers. Many of those who use cash use ATMs to obtain their cash. As institutions in a society change infrequently and slowly, Fisher concluded that the velocity of money is constant in the short run, but can change gradually in the long run. Other factors can affect the velocity of money. For example, the more frequent the pay period, the higher the velocity. An increase in transactions based on credit instead of cash might reduce the velocity. The velocity also depends on the habits of the citizens and their expectation about the state of the economy. While the anticipation of inflation induces people to hold less cash and spend it before the value erodes by inflation, the opposite will take place when a recession is anticipated. The constancy of velocity of money is a major part of the debate among the advocates of fiscal and monetary economics.[1,2]

The formulation of the quantity theory in equation 1.1 is known as the equation of exchange, because it explains the demand for money to pay for transactions or the exchanges of goods and services for money. Bartering, by contrast, does not involve money; therefore, it does not contribute toward demand for money. According to the equation of exchange, demand for money is a fraction of the national income. The fraction is actually equal to the inverse of the velocity of money. In order to demonstrate this more clearly, divide both sides of the equation of exchange by velocity

$$M = \frac{1}{V}PQ \qquad (1.2)$$

Rename the inverse of the velocity, as "k" yields the demand for money function

$$M^d = k(PQ) \qquad (1.3)$$

According to followers of the quantity theory of money, k is constant, because velocity of money is constant. Therefore, the number of transactions in the economy determines the *demand for money*. The value of the transactions is equal to the product of goods and services by their prices. For this purpose, it is more appropriate to use the "price level" instead of their "prices." A country that produces more goods and services—a rich country—demands more money, other things equal.

The equation of exchange is the foundation of the quantity theory of money. It indicates that the nominal income depends on the quantity of money, assuming that the velocity is constant. Interestingly, the quantity theory of money uses the demand for money equation to make statements on what would happen to the national income if the quantity of money (supply) changes. Another important thing to keep in mind is the fact that the association is between *nominal* national income and (the supply of) money, as opposed to *real* national income. Nominal values are not adjusted for inflation, whereas real values are.

Price *Versus* Output

The quantity theory states that an increase in (the supply of) money increases the nominal national income. The nominal national income is equal to P times Y, or PY. For the nominal national income to increase, either the price or the output should increase. National output is a function of the state of technology, invested capital, and employed labor force. Unless one or more of these factors change, output cannot change. With constant output, the only way nominal national income can increase is through an increase in the price level, which is the reason the term nominal instead of real national income is used. Let's make the convention of representing the variables that are constant with a superscript "c" to indicate they are constant.

$$P = \frac{MV^c}{Y^c} \tag{1.4}$$

Equation 1.4 indicates that an increase in (the supply of) money, other things equal, will only result in an increase in prices. In short, an increase in the supply of money causes inflation. Using mathematical formulations, it is easy to show that the quantity theory formula indicates that inflation is the difference in the percentage change in the supply of money and the percentage change in output.

Lemma

According to the quantity theory, the growth rate of inflation is equal to the difference in the growth rate of money and the growth rate of output.

It is worthwhile to point out that the demand for money from the perspective of quantity theory does not address the services that money provides. Even if this was an oversight in the writings of Hume[7] or Fisher,[3] it was deliberately omitted in Friedman,[8] because the fiscal policy had already questioned the quantity theory and provided alternative explanations for demand for money.

The quantity theory is expressed by equation 1.1 as a statement of fact, rather than theory. Obviously, there is sufficient money in circulation to pay for all the transactions that take place in an economy. The contribution of quantity theory to economics is its interpretation of this identity. The quantity theory raises the issue of what would happen if there were too much or too little money in the economy. As discussed earlier, the nation's output is a function of its factors of production, labor and capital, and the state of technology. Because followers of the quantity theory also assume constant or stable velocity, an increase in money supply would increase the price level. By analogy, if there is a decrease in the amount of available money, the price level must decrease. The former is known as *inflation*, and the latter is known as *deflation*. Neither recession nor inflation is desirable; however, there are two issues worth pointing out. First, equation 1.1 is a demand equation and not a supply equation. The equation can be rewritten as follows:

$$MV = PQ \qquad (1.5)$$

Advocates of quantity theory do not discuss the effect of a change in demand for money; rather, they focus on the effect of a change in the supply of money. Second, the customary definition of inflation and recession is based on production and demand. Using the transaction approach, a proportionate increase or decrease in the supply of money should have no effect on real output and the economy. Assume that a decision has been made to measure everything in pennies rather than dollars, effectively increasing the supply of money and all prices one-hundred fold. The change in the unit of measurement would not constitute inflation. This statement is not true when the actual amounts of all prices and incomes are increased proportionately, unless the wealth is also increased proportionately. This older version of quantity theory dates back to the early 1930s.

During the same time another way of interpreting the same equation was called cash-balance equation.

Cash-Balance Equation

The Cambridge equation is a representation of the quantity theory in terms of money, as presented in equation 1.3. It focuses on the demand for money rather than its supply.

$$M^d = k(PQ) \qquad (1.6)$$

In equation 1.6, k is nothing but the inverse of the velocity of money. Therefore, k represents the average duration for which money is held. If the velocity is 12, then each unit of money is held for about a month on average. This is also a mere expression of reality, void of theory. It identifies the duration of holding money for a given level of output, price level, and money on hand. Here too, the quantity of money equation is used to make a statement about the supply of money.

Neither the transaction nor cash-balance approach explains the reason for holding money nor the duration it is held. They do not provide any explanation on how the economy works. They do not even indicate whether people wanted to spend more or less than what they actually do. Discrepancy between the actual and the desired demand for money indicates what will happen to the economy. Whenever the economy is in disequilibrium, there will be corrective pressures to move it toward equilibrium. Although the ability to determine when and under what conditions the money market is out of equilibrium and to identify the direction necessary to move it toward equilibrium is very important, the statement that total transactions equal total payments is rather useless. It is more important to identify the conditions necessary for equilibrium than stating definitional identities. Whenever people have more or less of their assets in the form of money, there is disequilibrium. Some claim that the cash-balance approach is better than the equation of exchange.

CHAPTER 2

Transaction Theory of Demand for Money

The Transaction Theory

In Chapter 1, we pointed out that the output of the economy, Q in the equation of exchange, is a function of technology and factors of production, namely, labor and capital. Therefore, in the discussion of the relationship between money and prices, output and velocity were considered to be constant. This functional relationship for output does not preclude the possibility of recession. Because during a recession, the economy is not at full employment, Q would be at a level below the full-employment output. The requirement of full employment, which is more plausible in the long run than in the short run, is implicit in the quantity theory of demand for money. The change in the long run output is still a function of changes in technology, labor, and capital. However, the assumption of continuous full employment rules out the reality of short-run output fluctuations, which can be substantial as in the case of the Great Recession of 2008 when output dropped by 3.1% in current dollars.[1,2]

Restatement of the demand for money in the form of the cash balance equation $M^d = k(PQ)$ takes velocity out of the picture and instead makes demand for money a fraction of the value of output or national income. This allows another explanation for why people hold money when it has no direct utility and, unlike other types of assets, does not pay any interest. The idea that money does not provide direct utility implies that convenience in transactions does not have utility, which is false. Money facilitates exchange, and thus it provides valuable services as discussed in the introduction. However, in order for someone to hold money instead of an interest bearing asset, the utility of holding money must exceed the utility received from the resulting interest. Therefore, the *opportunity cost* of holding money—that is, the interest that could have been received from the highest paying forgone asset—is less than the utility of liquidity. Liquidity refers to the ease of spending money, in its different forms. This approach to demand for money is called the theory of *transaction demand for money*.

Once we acknowledge that money is demanded to meet transaction needs, we need to find out what governs the magnitude of demand for this purpose. One factor is income, which affects expenditures. Money is demanded to pay for transactions that are spread over the intervals of payment. Earned income is received on a periodic basis (e.g. once a week or monthly). Every few days a fraction of income for the period is spent as needed. The exact amount depends on one's income, taste, and habits. Elaborate models exist to calculate the exact amount under simplified assumptions.[3] Baumol and Tobin carefully use the term "transaction demand for money" instead of "demand for money."[4] The models determine how much cash one would hold using the need for transactions and the return to money, namely, the interest rate. This approach reflects the microeconomic view of demand for money. One way to obtain the macroeconomic demand for money is to add the individual demands for money.

Under the strict quantity theory principle, holding money would make sense for the purpose of expenditures. It would not make sense to hold assets in the form of currency earning no interest. There are several theories that explain this seemingly irrational behavior. Obviously, the return on investment and the cost of converting money to an interest bearing asset and back to money when needed are important factors as well. The former is called interest rate, and the latter is "shoe leather cost" at one time, implying that going to the bank to convert money into an interest bearing asset would wear the sole of the shoe.

A change in any of the following affects velocity:

a. Frequency of payment
b. Form of transactions (e.g. an increase in the use of credit cards or the ability to write checks against savings accounts directly)
c. Interest rate
d. Information

e. Information cost

f. Risk

Velocity and Interest Rate

Keynes argues that holding liquid funds for the purpose of transaction is responsive to changes in expenditure levels, but not the interest rate.[5] In other words, transaction demand for money is "elastic" with respect to the level of expenditures and "inelastic" with respect to interest rates.

Definition

The demand for a good or service is said to be elastic if the proportionate change in quantity demanded is greater than the proportionate change in the price of the good.

Baumol and Tobin use this view to address the effect of a change in expenditure on velocity.[3,4] In another study, Baumol also calculates an optimal cash balance holdings using the same concept.[6] Let us examine the effect of a change in the interest rate on velocity. Assume a person earns $48,000 per year and is paid monthly, thus earning $4,000 per month. For simplicity, assume there is "no tax," "social security," or other deductions. Alternatively, the discussion can be based on the net income, in the presence of such deductions and transfers. Assuming a uniform daily expenditure, the necessary cash for transaction is 1/30th of the income, or $133.33 per day. Since at the beginning of the month the person has $4,000 and at the end of the month has zero dollars, therefore, the average money balance is (4,000 + 0)/2 = $2,000. The only reason for this assumption is the ease of computation. For any other income expenditure pattern the weighted average can be used to obtain the average money balance.[7] The velocity of money is equal to annual income divided by the average monthly cash balance. For this example, the velocity is $48,000/$2,000 = 24.

In the presence of an interest bearing asset the person can lend the unused portion of his money to earn additional income. Assume the prevailing interest rate is 2%. To reduce the "shoe leather effect" the person lends only half of his monthly income for 15 days. The daily consumption expenditure remains equal to 1/30th of the income, or $133.33 per day because he is holding half of his income in the form of money, his average cash balance is halved, and his holding is $1,000 instead of $2,000. Therefore, the velocity of money is doubled as a result of halving the cash holding: $48,000/$1,000 = 48, instead of 24. Decreasing the cash holdings by half doubled the velocity, as expected.

To calculate the interest earned, recall that one half of the income ($2,000) is lent for one-half of the month at the rate of 2%. The interest equals (0.5 × 0.02 × 2,000 = $2) per month or $240 per year. If the trouble of going through lending is worth the $20, he will lend; otherwise, he will carry cash. According to Baumol, the amount of cash holding is directly related to the square root of the volume of transactions and brokerage fees and inversely related to the square root of the interest rate. The exact relation is provided in equation 2.1.[6]

$$M = \sqrt{\frac{2cY}{i}} \qquad (2.1)$$

where M is the cash holding per period, c is the transaction cost, Y is income per period, and i is the interest rate of the asset. Equation 2.1 can also be written as follows:

$$M = \sqrt{2c}\sqrt{\frac{Y}{i}} \qquad (2.2)$$

Equation 2.2 can be converted to the demand for money for transaction purposes by equation 2.3, where P stands for the price level.

$$M^d = \sqrt{2c}\sqrt{\frac{Y}{i}}P \qquad (2.3)$$

The *demand for money for transaction* purpose is a nonlinear function of transactions. Because the demand for money for transaction purpose depends on the square root of the transactions, there is an economy of scale in holding cash balances as the volume of transactions increases. Someone who earns twice as much as another person does not carry twice as much cash. Instead he will carry $\sqrt{2}$ = 1.41 times more cash than the other person. If we could generalize this to a national aggregate, an increase in national income does not increase cash holding requirements proportionately.

In the above example, if the interest rate increases, earnings will also increase. In the previous example, if the interest rate increases to 3%, the income from interest becomes $30. In other words, the opportunity cost of holding cash increases. Therefore, a typical individual is more likely to convert his money to an interest bearing asset given an increase in interest income. Thus, the nuisance of converting assets becomes more bearable by more people. It is also possible to increase the frequency of transactions and instead of withdrawing $2,000 every two weeks withdrawing $1,000 each week, thus increasing average asset holdings and reducing average cash holdings. The result is increased earnings from interest and increased velocity. Therefore, there is a direct relationship between interest rate and velocity.[4]

An important contribution of the theory of transaction demand for money is that it disproves the claim of the classical quantity theory of money, which indicates that demand for money is proportionate to the level of transactions. With this and similar arguments by Keynes, Tobin, Baumol, and others, the foundations of quantity theory were shaken. As will be seen, these arguments have also been shown to have problems and are not entirely correct.

An important factor that affects the demand for money is that the cost of converting assets to cash and vice versa reduces with technology. In the twenty-first century, it is possible to shift assets from one form to another electronically without a trip to a special broker or a bank. Therefore, part of the transaction cost is eliminated. By contrast, the suppliers of brokerage services have much lower transaction costs while they can handle larger volumes of transactions. The job that once required a building, office furniture, and other overhead can be performed through a single computer. Thus, the labor cost per transaction is declined. The cost savings allows the institution to reduce the transaction cost c, which according to the preceding discussion, reduces the demand for money for transaction purposes and increases the holding of assets in an interest bearing form. Because the use of technology has affected the nature of the need for holding currency, it is not clear as to whether the velocity of money increases as predicted previously. This could be an interesting empirical research topic.

It is important not to lose sight of the fact that we are still addressing the same motive for demanding money as in the quantity theory. Differences are seen in the point of emphasis, the assumptions, and, hence, the conclusion. For example, the quantity theory assumes that the velocity of money is constant and concludes that any increase in money supply, other things equal, increases prices only. The conclusion depends on the idea that supply and demand for money must be equal at the equilibrium. Note that the quantity theory only uses the transaction needs for money to explain the demand for money, whereas Keynes and his followers provide different justifications for demand for money based on different motives. Here the transaction motive is still the point of focus. Tobin, for example, focuses on the relationship between interest rates and demand for money and demonstrates there is an inverse relationship between the two.[4] He rewrites the equation of exchange in terms of velocity and concludes that as the interest rate changes, other things equal, the velocity has to change.

$$v = \frac{PQ}{M} \qquad (2.4)$$

As demonstrated previously, there is an inverse relationship between interest rate and demand for money; an increase in interest rate increases the opportunity cost of holding money, therefore, the demand for money declines, subsequently increasing the velocity. This is the case of simple algebra. Any number (e.g. PQ) divided by a smaller number, such as new lower demand, yields larger results, which is the velocity. Keynes and Tobin provide more complicated formulations of the concept, but the idea is the same.

CHAPTER 3

Portfolio Balances

Introduction

Early economists studying the demand for money focused on the transaction motive. Keynes pointed out that there are at least three motives for demand for money: transaction, precautionary, and speculative.[1] In Chapter 2, we discussed the transaction motive of demand for money from a non-quantity theory perspective. In this chapter, we will focus on the speculative motive for demand for money. Analyzing the demand for money from the perspective of different motives provides an insight about the relationship between key financial variables such as interest rate and velocity with money.

In the absence of inflation, money does not lose its value, but some assets, such as treasury bonds, earn interest in addition to maintaining their value. The value of some assets such as stocks fluctuates over time. Yet other securities pay dividends and appreciate in value as well. The type, timing, and nature of payment determine the specific name for the resulting income, such as interest, yield, or dividend. Timing of the action is important. In order to make profit from these financial instruments one should buy when their prices are low and sell when their prices are high. Unfortunately, it is not possible for everyone to buy low and sell high. However, the expectation of what will happen to a specific stock in the future is different for different people. The difference stems from differences in information, one's willingness to take risks, and the availability of other options or needs. Furthermore, the amount of cash available to different people varies over time. When a transaction takes place, the exchange price is the same for the buyer and the seller. Therefore, expectations about the future, the availability of resources, and information about the asset must be different for buyers and sellers. The seller must expect the asset price to fall in the future, while the buyer must believe the opposite. Similarly, the seller might need cash, believe that another asset provides higher return, or need to change his portfolio mix, making it reasonable to sell his assets; the opposite must be true for the buyer. Disparity of needs, expectations, opportunities, and information make it possible for people to buy and sell assets at a given price. The prices of traded assets fluctuate in response to the expectations and needs of buyers and sellers. When there are more buyers than sellers, the prices increase, while the opposite is true when the number of sellers exceeds that of buyers.

The expectation of what will happen in the future is an important factor in the decision to buy or sell assets. An expectation of a price decline initiates a sale, even if the current price is below the price of the original purchase. In such a case, the asset holder is minimizing his loss. We deliberately avoid using the word "profit" because it has a different meaning in economics. As will be explained in Chapter 8, the correct term is "earning income from assets". An anticipation of price appreciation would prompt a purchase, which requires having cash on hand to take advantage of the opportunity. There are two ways to have sufficient cash to make the transaction. First, one could hold extra cash balance over and beyond the amount necessary to meet transaction needs. Second, one could sell or liquidate other assets to obtain cash. Keynes termed this as *portfolio motive*.[1] Changes in economic condition and/or stock prices affect the amount of money that people choose to hold according to the portfolio motive, which changes velocity of money and invalidates the constancy of velocity, as assumed by the advocates of the quantity theory. Furthermore, because converting assets to money in anticipation of possible bargains in the stock market is costly and time consuming, the decision must be made when possible and appropriate. To convert a low-yield asset into a higher yield asset, it must first be converted into money, which is then exchanged for the new asset. Thus, decisions to increase the amount of cash on hand are not made at regular intervals, implying a nonconstant velocity of money.

Nominal *Versus* Real

The equation of exchange is expressed in equation 3.1.

$$MV = PQ \qquad (3.1)$$

Equation 3.1 states that the product of the quantity of money and its velocity equals the nominal spending in the economy, represented by the *nominal value* of transactions, which equals price times output. However, the quantity theory of money is based on the *real money balances*. Rearranging the equation of exchange in the following form presents the real money balances.

$$\frac{M}{P} = \left(\frac{1}{V}\right)Q \tag{3.2}$$

This is the same formula as equation 1.2 in Chapter 1. Dividing nominal quantity of money by price level results in the real quantity of money. Economists are interested in the real factors, rather than the nominal, because it is the purchasing power of the money that matters. There are several variables that affect the demand for real money balances.

Income and Wealth

People and firms with low income tend to keep the majority of their earnings in cash because they depend on most or all of their income to pay for current consumption or transactions. As income and earnings increase, it is possible to hold part of the income in interest bearing assets to take advantage of the extra earnings. Therefore, as income increases, relatively less money is held as cash. It is important to understand that as the income of people and firms increases, the demand for money and the amount of assets held in cash increases, but at a slower rate than the rise in income.

Wealth is accumulated income. The existence of wealth implies that some income was not spent. Similar to income, as wealth increases, a larger portion of it is held in interest bearing assets. However, it is not clear why anybody would hold wealth in the form of cash. Keynes argues that as wealth increases, the demand for currency increases, but at a decreasing rate.

Expected Returns

The opportunity cost of holding cash increases when the return to other assets increases. Therefore, as the interest rate increases, the incentive to convert cash into other assets increases and the demand for liquidity decreases; thus, the velocity of money increases. As discussed in Chapter 2, the price of higher earnings is the loss of convenience and relatively low risk of holding currency. Each individual and firm places different valuation on convenience, risk, and earnings and responds differently to economic changes. However, as the interest rate increases, the demand for money should decrease.

Asset Risk and Liquidity

Different assets have different risks. Interest bearing assets usually have a higher risk than holding cash. The speed and cost of changing assets to cash differs as well. Real estate, for example, is more difficult to liquidate than U.S. bonds. The transaction cost of converting real estate to cash is approximately 6–7% for residential properties and approximately 10–15% for commercial properties. This is higher than the typical costs associated with converting many other assets into cash. Usually, greater time and cost of converting an asset to cash entails higher yields.

The risk for holding assets other than money is also higher than holding cash. As the risk increases, the expected return to the asset must increase in order to entice households and firms to part with their cash. Financial innovations that make it easier to convert an interest bearing asset into cash reduce the demand for holding cash. There are numerous arrangements that allow converting bonds, stocks, and even home equity into cash.

Other Factors Affecting Demand for Liquidity

Holding cash provides an anonymity that is not possible with most other assets. It is necessary to provide personal information, such as social security number, earnings, or wealth, when purchasing financial assets. This reveals your wealth and net worth. Some people place a value on the anonymity of cash in addition to the convenience it provides. It would be careless to deposit the earnings from illegal activities into a traceable asset. The earnings from traceable sources, such as stocks and bonds, are taxable. Therefore, the demand for money will be affected by changes in the level of illegal activities, preferences for anonymity, and tax laws.

Speculative Motive

Keynes used the term *Speculative Motive* to describe the aforementioned reasons for holding cash.[1] For simplification, he used bonds as representative for interest bearing assets. Therefore, he limited his argument to two assets, money that earns no interest and bonds that do. The expected return to bonds is determined by the interest rate. In order to obtain capital, firms, cities, and the Federal Government issue bonds. In order to convince people to purchase bonds—to part with their cash—the interest rate must be higher than the current interest rate, as the current interest rate is the market clearing equilibrium rate. Let us assume there is a zero-coupon bond with a par value of $100.00 that is trading for $97.00. At this market clearing price, the return to the bond is (100–97)/97 = 3.09%, which is the same as receiving 3.09% interest. Suppose that either the interest rate increased or that the government is issuing new bonds that yield 5% interest. No one will buy the existing bond at $97.00 because the effective interest rate of 3.09% is less than the market interest rate. The demand for the existing bond will decrease and its price will fall. The price decline will continue until the interest rate on the existing bond equals the new interest rate. The new price for the existing bond is $95.24, which yields a return that is almost 5%. Therefore, as the interest rate increases, the price of a bond decreases and vice versa. The advocates of the quantity theory do not dispute the inverse relationship between the price of interest bearing assets and the interest rate. Keynes continues the analysis by pointing out that in order to buy the new bond to take advantage of the higher interest rate, people must hold some extra cash to satisfy the speculative motive. The holding of extra cash affects the demand for money. Furthermore, when the cash is spent on the new bond, the person is holding less cash. The remaining money must churn faster in order to pay for all the transactions, thus increasing the velocity of money. Thus, the transaction motive effectively challenges the quantity theory assumption of constant velocity.

Adding the other two motives for demand for money, Keynes concluded that liquidity preference depends on real income, Y, and interest rate on other assets. Keynes used the real demand for money, which is obtained by dividing the nominal demand for money, M, by the price level, P.

$$\frac{M}{PY} = \frac{L(Y,i)}{Y} \qquad (3.3)$$

It is expected that an increase in income and transactions will increase the demand for real balances. Therefore, the relationship between M/P and Y is direct. On the contrary, as explained earlier, there is an inverse relationship between real demand for money and interest rate.

In his original work, Keynes included public expectations of the normal interest rate. If the interest rate was higher than expected, the public would expect it to drop, and thus acted accordingly. An expectation of a drop in interest rate means that the bond price is expected to rise. Consequently, it makes sense to buy bonds now and sell them when the price goes up. The opposite occurs when the expectation is that the interest rates will increase, because it is below the expected rate.

Dividing both sides of equation 3.3 by Y and noting that the left hand side of the new equation is the inverse of the velocity results in the following:

$$\frac{1}{V} = \frac{M}{PY} = \frac{L(Y,i)}{Y} \qquad (3.4)$$

When income increases, velocity increases, but when the interest rate increases, the opportunity cost of holding money increases. Therefore, when interest rates rise, the demand for bonds increases and that of money decreases, hence the velocity decreases.

CHAPTER 4

Money Theories and Estimation

Introduction

Keynes' liquidity preference approach to money demand shook the foundations of the classical quantity theory. For example, Keynes challenged the classical quantity theory's explanation of the consequence of the effects of an increase in the supply of money. Keynes' theory demonstrates that velocity need not be, and in fact is not, constant; and demand for money depends on the interest rate, as well as income. This and other components of Keynes' theory provides an alternative solution to the Great Depression of 1929. Over time, it seemed that the quantity theory was dead. Fiscal policy became the dominant economic policy of the pre- and post-World War II era, at least until Friedman revived monetary policy.[1]

Permanent Income Hypothesis

Friedman revived the quantity theory by focusing on the determinants of asset demand.[1] Friedman used the M2 definition of money instead of M1. Chapter 6 provides definitions of types of money such as M_1 and M_2. He stated that one's demand for real money is also a function of one's wealth. Portfolio investment decisions depend on wealth and affect the demand for real money balances. The word *real* is not used in contrast to *fake* or *unreal* rather it is used in contrast to *nominal*. Real money is the ratio of nominal money to price, to account for inflation. The demand for nominal money is equal to the demand for real money times inflation. Friedman used the concept of the permanent income hypothesis, Y^*, to represent wealth.

In the permanent income hypothesis, one's transitory income has little effect on portfolio balance decisions. Under this hypothesis, the demand for real money is a function of the difference between the return on money and interest bearing assets, as well as the difference between the return on money and expected inflation. The expected returns on assets and money are actually the same as their opportunity costs and are shown by i and i_M, respectively. Expected inflation is shown by π^e.

$$\frac{M}{P} = L(Y^*, i - i_M, \pi^e - i_M) \qquad (4.1)$$

The direct relationship between the demand for money and income only pertains to one's permanent income and not one's transitory income. There is an inverse relationship between the demand for money and the opportunity cost of holding it. There is also an inverse relationship between one's expected income, minus the opportunity cost of holding cash, and the demand for money.

Keynes' and Friedman's Views of Demand for Money

The models proposed by Keynes and Friedman both relate the demand for money to portfolio investment behavior. However, the main difference is that the latter brings the focus on the long-run back into the demand for money. Friedman actually states that transitory income has absolutely no effect on the portfolio balances of households. Friedman explicitly includes inflation in the demand function, thus returning the link between price level and money back into the demand for money, as in the traditional quantity theory. However, Patinkin questions the claim that Friedman belongs to the quantity theory tradition.[2] While Keynes' portfolio uses bonds as a representative interest bearing asset, Friedman's portfolio includes money, bonds, equities, and durable goods.

The nominal values of all assets in Friedman's model increase with inflation. Housing is the most important of the durable goods in the model. In response to anticipated inflation, households begin protecting their assets by transferring them from money to other assets whose values increase with inflation. This is because the real value of money erodes with inflation. Friedman's model uses the M2 definition of money, part of which earns interest. By contrast, Keynes' M1 money does not earn any interest; therefore, holding money deprives the holder from earning interest, while holding bonds is a source of income. In Friedman's model, the return to money includes some earned interest through the time deposits portion of M2, plus all the implicit benefits accrued to the money at the financial institutions, such as processing checks and paying bills. Both models agree that the demand for money depends on the differences in the return on different interest bearing assets and money. However, the major difference in this regard is the value that the two models attach to the outcome. Unlike Keynes, Friedman believes that the differences on the earnings are small enough not to have a significant impact on the demand for money. Thus, on one hand, by using the M2 definition of money, he makes the interest rate earned by money greater than zero, but on the other hand, he claims that the difference in this rate and the rate of return on other assets is negligible, thus, eroding the foundations of the liquidity preference model. Friedman was able to revive the quantity theory, but the contributions of Keynes are still apparent in the modern formulation of the demand for real money balances.

The Modern Version of Quantity Theory

In the modern version of quantity theory, money is considered to be one of many different assets held by a household or a capital good owned by a business. Money is combined with other resources, such as labor, to produce goods and services. In these contexts, money is a commodity that provides direct utility. Under the classical quantity theory, money had only indirect utility. Its utility was derived from the utility of other goods and services that it bought. The demand for money, thus, stemmed from the services it provided for the household or business enterprise. It was necessary to discard both the approach of using different motives for holding money and the idea of indirect utility. The new approach to the quantity theory treats money the same as any other commodity with direct utility, thus making it possible to apply conventional demand theory to money demand. The determinants of demand for money are now identifiable as similar to those factors that drive demand for other goods and services.

The demand for money now includes a component to account for the demand for real money to satisfy transactions. This portion of the money demand is also influenced by expectations about the future. An anticipated decline in next year's purchases will diminish the demand for money and allow people to obtain assets to earn interest. An increase in substitute means of payments, such as credit cards, savings deposits with debit cards or check writing allowances, reduces the demand for real money balances. The expected return on different assets that provide financial rewards—after correcting for cost, liquidity, and risk—influences the demand for real money.

The Role of Wealth

In the theory of consumption demand, Friedman identifies the main factors affecting the demand for money for either a household or a business enterprise.

$$\frac{M}{P} = f(i_m, i_b, i_e, p_r, W, n) \tag{4.2}$$

where i_m is the rate of return on money; i_b is the rate of return on bonds; i_e is the rate of return on equities; p_r is the rate of change of the price index over time; W is wealth; n is the ratio of nonhuman to human wealth.

The wealth variable in this formulation is the constraint of the model, somewhat similar to the role that income plays in a demand function. Human wealth is the same as the term *human capital* that has become more customary in economic models since the 1980s. In economics, wealth is the discounted present value of future earnings. In this regard, human wealth is the present value of future earnings. Human wealth can be augmented to increase future earnings through increased education. Current literature uses the term *human capital* synonymous with education. An increase in education increases human wealth, indicating a direct relationship between the two. Human wealth increases through either formal education, or learning by doing (i.e. informal experience), over the years. The larger the share of human wealth is compared to nonhuman wealth, the higher the demand for liquid balances. This is because it is difficult to convert human wealth to money. In order to use the stream of future returns to human wealth, one must work and earn income.

Possession of human wealth increases income, which in turn causes an increase in demand for real balances. For an unemployed person, human wealth is similar to having one's assets in the form of the M1 definition of money that earns zero return, which implies that highly educated people maintain larger sums of money—or for Friedman, the M2 definition of money, is a testable hypothesis.

This demand for money function is universal and explains the demand function for both households and business firms. The variable, human wealth to nonhuman wealth, takes the value of zero when dealing with businesses. The procedure to rewrite the demand for money function in terms of velocity is the same as the one discussed in Chapter 3 and elsewhere. Multiplying both sides of the equation by income, rearranging the terms, and equating the nominal money demand to the nominal supply expresses the stated relationship in terms of the velocity of money. The determinants of velocity are the same as the determinants of the demand for real money, which vary depending on whether the quantity theory or the portfolio and transaction demand for money theory is used.

Replacing income with wealth is a major shift in paradigm. The new quantity theory provides ample opportunity for testing the validity of the model and its variables. Friedman provided an empirical study using statistical analysis to support his theory.[1] One criticism to his analysis is that it seems that he changed the variables, such as money, to obtain statistically significant results. Consequently, the question of whether wealth or income is a better explanatory variable has become important, and the subject of numerous studies since then. Similar studies have been devoted to the broader question of which model is more appropriate and better able to explain the money demand behavior of the public, the relative importance of each of the three interest rates used in Friedman's model, and the structural stability of the model. Interestingly, Friedman himself could not find any empirical support for the importance of any of the three interest rates he includes in the model. The result could mean that either the model is incorrect, the method is incorrect, or that the model is specified incorrectly. As his attempt to find a statistically significant relationship between the three interest rates and velocity was also unsuccessful, Friedman dismissed both outcomes as irrelevant to his theory and instead placed the importance on the relationship between the demand for real money and permanent income, which is a measure of long-term income.

We can compare the concept of permanent income to the notion of expected (long term) income, while perceiving transitory income as simply the noise or the random error. In statistical analysis, the expected value of any random error is zero. The term *expected* is used in its statistical context meaning the average, or the theoretically acceptable outcome.[3] For example, when flipping a fair coin on a hard surface, the expected probability of the coin landing heads-up is 50%. The word *expect* is not meant to imply what is imagined or assumed, nor is it meant to imply what is demanded or required. In regression analysis, a common statistical tool, the object is to weed out the noise or random error to find the theoretically prevailing relationship between two variables such as the demand for money and income.[4] In the end, Friedman ignores all the other variables that he introduced in his permanent income hypothesis and instead focused solely on the measure of permanent income as a proxy for wealth.

The inclusion of the variables Friedman used in his model was essential in reducing the importance of the variables in the portfolio balances of Keynes. Friedman had to abandon the three measures of interest, due to lack of statistical significance. He also had to drop the human wealth variable in the absence of an appropriate measure of human wealth. Later research has used measures of educational attainment as proxies for human capital, such as average or median years of schooling or the percentage of the population with certain educational degrees, such as college. These human capital measures could be used as proxies for human wealth. There are numerous issues in using educational attainment for human wealth; however, the discussion of these implications is beyond the scope of the present book. An important point to take away from this discussion is that the use of proxies for variables can cause serious statistical problems, and therefore lead to difficulty in finding support even for highly influential economic theories, which was demonstrated repeatedly during the final decades of the twentieth century.

SECTION II

Supply of Money

CHAPTER 5

Federal Reserve System

Where Does Money Come From?

The public has a notion about money that is often limited to currency, both coins and bills. Because economists need to have a precise definition of every concept to build appropriate theories that explain the economy, the previous chapters provided several different descriptions of money. In summary, anything that fulfills the different functions of money is money. Different types of money are defined based on the degree of their liquidity. Chapter 6 provides concrete definitions for different types of money.

Money consists of both currency and noncurrency forms. Paper money, which is also called the Federal Reserve Note or the United States Banknote, is printed by the Bureau of Engraving and Printing. Until 1913, the Treasury Department was responsible for making all decisions to print money for the country. The amount of money in the economy, or the money supply, has since been controlled by the Federal Reserve Bank System (the Fed). The Fed must initiate the process before the money can be printed by the Treasury Department, which is disbursed into the economy by the Fed. The Fed buys Treasury bonds in the possession of financial institutions, commercial banks, individual people, and other entities, such as municipalities, states, and foreign governments. The Federal Reserve Bank System was created by the Federal Reserve Act of 1913. The authority and functions of the Fed have been modified over the years.[1]

As explained in previous chapters, the amount of money demanded for daily economic transactions is a function of the output of the economy, the total amount of transactions, the value of the currency, and the velocity of money. The need for new money stems from an increase in economic activity and population, loss of currency due to wear or misplacement, damage, or deliberate exclusion from circulation, such as stuffing it in a mattress. The money that is created to replace the aforementioned losses of money is not considered new money.

Money can be created without actually *printing* new bills or minting new coins. Chapter 12 explains this procedure. It is important to know the different types of money and how they are generated, controlled, and distributed in order to be able to identify how much money is available in the economy. Understanding these concepts is necessary in order to determine whether there is sufficient money in the economy. If there is an insufficient amount of money to meet the needs of the economy, there will be a recession. However, if there is too much money, inflation will result. The Federal Reserve Bank system is responsible for taking appropriate steps to assure that sufficient amount of money is available in the economy. When necessary, it must take corrective steps, in the right direction and by the appropriate amount, to synchronize the stock of money with existing economic conditions. In general, it is expected to take steps that will help move the economy in the desired direction to achieve policy goals that would result in a prosperous economy.

The main money creation function of the Fed, however, is its ability to generate money by augmenting the existing money supply through the process of money recirculation, which is described in more detail in Chapter 12. This occurs through changing the reserve requirements of commercial banks, changing interest rates, buying and selling bonds, and similar activities that are collectively known as money market management and are part of monetary policy.[2] The process of how new money is created through the banking system through the Federal Reserve's monetary policies—specifically implementing open market transactions—is beyond the scope of this text.

Bankers have known for centuries that they could not lend all the money that is deposited by owners of funds, because bank customers might request withdrawals from their deposits from time to time. By contrast, keeping the entire amount of deposits in the vault is unnecessary because a large portion of deposits stay for extended periods. Estimating the exact amount of cash necessary to meet the demand for withdrawals is not easy, and there were times that there was not sufficient cash in hand to meet the withdrawal requests. In such cases the word spreads rapidly, the public panic and rush to the bank to get their money, and create a *run* on the bank. Often, public panic in one town spreads to the neighboring towns and states. In 1907, the run on banks across the United States was widespread and momentous. Consequently, the Congress established the National Monetary Commission in 1908 to review the banking system and make recommendations for reform. The Congress later passed the Federal Reserve Act of 1913 "to provide for the establishment of Federal Reserve banks, to furnish an elastic currency, to afford means of rediscounting commercial papers, to establish a more effective supervision of banking in the United States, and for other purposes."[3]

Federal Reserve System

Until the late nineteenth century, the banking system in the United States was unorganized and private. Private Banks, in pursuit of maximizing profits, tended to loan excessive portion of the deposited money and at times they did not have sufficient cash to meet their obligations. Banks generate their revenue by borrowing and lending money. They charge higher interest on the money they lend than the interest they pay when they borrow. The difference in the two interest rates is known as the *net interest margin*. The interest rates paid by and received by the bank are a function of the supply and demand for the loanable funds, the reputation of the bank, and the existing economic conditions. These lending functions, which determine the interest rates utilized by the private banks, have not changed over time and are still the same in principle. The Federal Reserve Act ended the era of completely free market banking and many other aspects of that banking system as well as the period of frequent runs on banks. The Federal Reserve System did not eliminate bank failures completely. In fact between 1934 and 2013 there were over 4,000 bank failures. However, the majority of these failures were isolated and unrelated, with three exceptions: the Great Depression from 1929 to 1933, the Savings and Loans Crisis from 1984 to 1991, and the Sub-Prime Crisis of 2007–2011.[4,5] The Sub-Prime Crisis resulted in the Great Recession of 2007–2009. The Savings and Loan (S & L) Crisis is an interesting case as it demonstrates the problems of too little as well as too much government regulation and involvement. Because of several reasons, most notably the rapid increase in the price of oil due to Iranian Revolution in 1979, the short-term interest rates increased substantially causing numerous problems. These include the financial stress on S & L that had outstanding long-term loans at low interest rates and were unable to attract funds for their operations. Consequently S & L were deregulated in 1980. Part of the deregulation involved a reduction in the oversight of operations. This and other banking deregulations during the 1980s resulted in S & L Crisis that lasted from 1984 to 1991. The current authorities and responsibilities of the Fed have evolved through varying legislation, some to limit the scope of the Fed's existing authorities, and others to clarify or to augment them.[1,6]

The nineteenth century banking system of the United States, and for that matter most of the world, is a good example of how the free market could fail making a regulated banking system necessary. The asymmetry of information, which will be discussed in more detail in Chapter 10, is a major contributing factor supporting the need for regulation. Like other complex phenomenon, it is unreasonable to expect a simple explanation for the failure of the banking system. Similarly, it is just as unreasonable to expect simplistic solutions to remedy the problem. The free market would work, provided the necessary conditions are met. In the case of the banking system, several of the necessary conditions are difficult to meet in practice. For example, in many cases, information is not available to both the suppliers and the demanders of the service, although financial information on banks is more commonly available than those of other financial institutions. Furthermore, because the money market and its functions are complex, it is necessary to have some expertise in comprehending the available information. The knowledge of the general public and professionals in the field is not comparable, which allows for people with more knowledge to take advantage of those without it when the components of the system change. As components of the system change constantly, it is necessary to have regulations and monitors to make sure the system works properly. A banking system without regulation is comparable to a country without driving laws. Although traffic lights slow and at times stop traffic in one direction or the other, removing them would cause chaos. Similarly, regulations in the banking and monetary system increase transaction costs and might cause a seemingly unnecessary slowdown in the flow of economic activities; however, these regulations are a step in the right direction to avoid chaos, bankruptcies, recurring and frequent economic swings, both recessionary and inflationary, and other economic calamities. By contrast, too many regulations can stifle economic activities. Striking the appropriate balance is a formidable task.

A Banking Federation

The *Federal Reserve System*, as its name indicates, is a federated system, consisting of a central agency called the Board of Governors and 12 regional Federal Reserve banks located in Boston, New York, Philadelphia, Cleveland, Richmond, Atlanta, Chicago, St. Louis, Minneapolis, Kansas City, Dallas, and San Francisco.[3] The federated system provides some independence to individual regional Federal Reserve banks, but also imposes some restrictions upon them to make the system work more homogenously. Part of the system's responsibilities is to regulate and oversee specific financial institutions and the dissemination of information about the economy and its financial matters.

By far, the most important part of the system is the *Federal Open Market Committee* (FOMC); open market activities are the subject of monetary policy.[2] The FOMC consists of the members of the Board of Governors, the president of the Federal Reserve Bank of New York, and, on a rotating basis, presidents of four other Federal Reserve banks. The Federal Reserve Board of Governors estimates the necessary interest rate that would accomplish a particular monetary objective, known as monetary policy. Federal Reserve banks charge that interest rate when commercial banks need to borrow from their funds. Commercial banks borrow from the Federal Reserve banks' funds when their cash reserves decline to below the required percentage of their total deposits, which is also set by the Federal Reserve Board of Governors.

The seven members of the Board of Governors are appointed by the President of the United States for one term and confirmed by the United States Senate. Each member serves for 14 years. Although the Federal Reserve System is subject to oversight by the United States Congress, its decisions are final and not subject to approval by anyone in the executive branch of government. This is done in order to isolate it from the political pressures and influences that follow the two- and four-year cycles of elections.

The Fed's responsibilities include exercising the monetary policy to maximize employment, to stabilize prices, and to regulate the long-term interest rates. The Fed regulates commercial banks to maintain a healthy financial system, to protect the credit rights of their customers, to stabilize the financial system, to moderate risk, to provide financial services to the United States government and depository institutions, and to facilitate the nation's payments system. The international responsibilities of the Chairman of the Fed include participation as a member of the board of the Bank for International Settlements (BIS), the Board of Governors of the International Monetary Fund, and the National Advisory Council on International Monetary and Financial Policies. The Chairman is also part of a United States delegation to the meetings of the finance ministers and central bank governors of the seven largest industrial countries (G7). Additionally, the Fed participates in an annual BIS meeting in Basel, Switzerland, and in the Organization for Economic Co-operation and Development meeting in Paris, France. This brief introduction does not do justice to all the responsibilities that the Chairman of the Fed has to attend to, let alone in managing the functions of the Fed. Readers interested in the activities of the Fed should refer to The Federal Reserve Board report.[3] In most countries, the central bank fulfills the Federal Reserve responsibilities.

Publications

The main publications of the Board are the *Federal Reserve Bulletin*, the monthly *Statistical Supplement*, and the monthly publications of the Federal Reserve Regulatory Service. The first two provide detailed statistics about the economy and the financial system's activities. The latter provides materials pertaining to the supervisory and regulatory responsibilities of the Fed. The Board also publishes research papers about economics, finance, and banking.

Every year the Board must be audited by a major public accounting firm, in addition to periodic reviews by the *Government Accountability Office (GAO)*. These audits usually focus on specific activities and functions of the Board. The results of all such reviews are reported in the *Annual Report* of the Board. The reports are submitted to the Congress during the second quarter of each year. The review does not include monetary policy, which is exempt from audit by GAO, as it is monitored directly by the Congress. Monetary policy activities are submitted through the semiannual *Monetary Policy Report* to the Congress.

State banks are not required to be members of the Federal Reserve System, but those that are members are supervised and regulated by the Board in a similar manner to bank holding companies and national banks. The Board also oversees the foreign activities of member banks, the activities of foreign banks in the United States, and the implication of the *Edge Act* and agreement corporations. These corporations are limited-purpose institutions that are engaged in a foreign banking business.

Some of the Federal Reserve banks have branches, which as of 2013, totaled 25. The combined system operates a nationwide payments system, distributes currency, supervises and regulates member banks and bank holding companies, and serves as a banker for the United States Treasury. Each of the 12 Reserve Banks acts as a depository for the banks in its own district. The Board of Governors controls the activities of the 12-member banks and their branches and approves the budget for each of the 12-member banks. The law requires that each of the 12 Reserve Banks have a Board of Directors with nine members chosen from outside the bank, consisting of individuals from industrial, agricultural, commercial, and banking industries within the region. The Board of Directors of each Federal Reserve Bank is divided into three groups, referred to as Class A, Class B, and Class C, each with three members. The members of Class A are chosen from commercial banks within the region, whereas the members of Class B and Class C are selected from nonbank industries. Members of Congress cannot serve as directors. The directors of Class C are barred from owning stock in a bank or bank holding company, whereas the members of Class B and Class C are barred from being an officer, director, or even an employee of a bank or a bank holding company. The member commercial banks in each district elect Class A and Class B directors, whereas the Board of Governors appoints the directors for Class C, one as chairman and another as deputy chairman.

Most efforts of the members of the Boards of Directors, as with other members of the Federal Reserve System, are focused on collecting information to measure the economic pulse of the nation and to provide the necessary data to allow the Fed to identify the appropriate response through open market operations. All information is available to the public and is published in the Beige Book. The Beige Book becomes available about two weeks before an FOMC meeting. One of the responsibilities of the Board of each of the 12 primary Federal Reserve banks is biweekly discount rate recommendations.

The Federal Reserve is a revenue generating agency. The income is from the interest on United States government securities obtained through open market transactions, interest earned on foreign currency investments, and service fees for check clearing, funds transfers, as well as automated clearinghouse activities. Not all of the Fed's revenue goes into the United States Treasury. The Fed pays for its own expenses first. The list of incomes and expenses of the Federal Reserve Bank and its audited financial report are published in the *Annual Report of the Board of Governors.*

The Federal Financial Institutions Examination Council coordinates the federal-level examinations of depository institutions. Its members are from the Federal Deposit Insurance Corporation, the Office of the Comptroller of the Currency, the National Credit Union Administration, the Office of Thrift Supervision, and the Board of Governors of the Federal Reserve System.

FOMC

Although this text will not include an in-depth treatment of monetary policy and how it functions, it is important to address the basic functions of the FOMC, because of its importance for the Fed in achieving monetary policy objectives.[2] The FOMC consists of the seven members of the Board of Governors and five of the 12 Reserve Bank presidents. Although the president of the Federal Reserve Bank of New York is a permanent member and the rest of the members serve for one year and rotate, this does not mean that the rest of the presidents of the Banks do not participate in discussions; only that they do not vote on policy decisions. The Congress has granted the FOMC the right to establish its own internal organization. Traditionally, the Chairman of the Board of Governors is chosen as the chairman of the FOMC, and the president of the Federal Reserve Bank of New York serves as the vice chairman. The FOMC meets eight times a year. Other meetings and communications are prevalent.

Advisory Committees

Three advisory committees assist the Federal Reserve System: the Federal Advisory Council, the Consumer Advisory Council, and the Thrift Institutions Advisory Council.

Federal Advisory Council

This council has 12 representatives from the banking industry and provides advice and consultation on all matters within the Board's jurisdiction. It meets four times a year, as mandated by the Federal Reserve Act of 1913. The meetings are on the first Friday of February, May, September, and December, and are held in Washington, D.C. The Federal Reserve chooses one person to represent its district on the Federal Advisory Committee. Each member usually serves three one-year terms, and the committee elects its own officers.

Consumer Advisory Council

The council, which was established in 1976, focuses on the Board's responsibilities as outlined in the Consumer Credit Protection Act. It also provides advice on matters of consumer financial services. The Council's three annual meetings, held in Washington D.C., are open to the public.

Thrift Institutions Advisory Council

In 1980, the Federal Reserve was charged with oversight of the thrift institutions and the Depository Institution Deregulation and Monetary Control Act. Consequently, the thrift institutions are subject to the Federal Reserve's regulations, and in return, they have access to the discount window. This council, unlike the other two, is not statutorily mandated, although it has similar functions and purposes as the other two councils. This Council meets three times a year with the Board of Governors in Washington D.C. The members of the Council, appointed by the Board of Governors for two years, are limited to the representatives of savings and loan institutions, credit unions, and mutual savings banks.

To expand inputs, the Federal Reserve Bank utilizes numerous advisory committees. The most important of these committees are the ones that advise on matters of agriculture, small business, and labor. Each of the 12 Reserve Banks has one such committee. The Board of Governors petitions the views of these committees twice a year.

Monetary Aggregates

In the literature, you will encounter monetary aggregates that are used in monetary policy. The monetary aggregates refer to different definitions of money, such as M1, M2, and M3. The primary differences between these definitions of the money stock are due to differences in what is considered money and also due to differences in the liquidity of different forms of money. We discussed these differences and different forms of money in the previous chapters. If you recall, there is a direct relationship between inflation and the supply of money. An increase in inflation requires more money to meet the transaction needs of the economy. Similarly, the relationship between economic growth and the need for money is also direct. A larger economy requires a greater supply of money to accommodate the increased amount of transactions. However, the relationship is neither one-to-one nor unidirectional. The relationship is not one-to-one due to the fact that the velocity of money is not necessarily constant, as assumed by the advocates of the classical quantity theory. The relationship is not unidirectional because a change in the supply of money can increase the size of the economy (i.e. the GDP), in the short run and price levels (i.e. inflation) in the long run. The former is more likely in the short run and the latter in the long run. The other factors that affect money, and hence monetary policy, are the interest rates and foreign exchange rates.

CHAPTER 6

Forms of Money
in the Economy

Types of Money

In the introduction, we pointed out that money has three properties. Money is a medium of exchange, a unit of account, and acts as a store of value. Next, we introduced the concept of what is considered money in modern economies. We also pointed out that there are several kinds of money with different levels of liquidity. *Liquidity* refers to the ease of spending different types of monetary assets. An asset is perfectly liquid if it can be converted to currency immediately, without any risk, loss of value, or cost. However, every type of money has some cost and risk compared to currency, as will become evident in this chapter. The complex economies that have developed since the Renaissance have created numerous monetary tools, each of which fulfills some, if not necessarily all of the functions of money. In order to determine the necessary amount of money in the economy, it is necessary to define money and all of the *near money* instruments precisely. An economy lacking a sufficient amount of money would face economic contractions, whereas an economy with too much money would suffer from inflation. Money in the economy can be compared to blood in the human body. To function properly, the economy requires the correct amount of money, just as a body requires the correct amount of blood.

M1 consists of (1) currency outside the U.S. Treasury, Federal Reserve banks, and the vaults of depository institutions; (2) traveler's checks of nonbank issuers; (3) demand deposits at commercial banks (excluding those amounts held by depository institutions, the U.S. government, and foreign banks and official institutions), less cash items in the process of collection and Federal Reserve float; and (4) other checkable deposits

(OCDs), consisting of negotiable order of withdrawal (NOW) and auto-matic transfer service accounts at depository institutions, credit union share draft accounts, and demand deposits at thrift institutions. A seasonally adjusted M1 is constructed by summing currency, traveler's checks, demand deposits, and OCDs, after each has been individually seasonally adjusted. Seasonal adjustments are procedures that reduce or eliminate fluctuations caused by changes in seasons rather than changes in economic factors.

Some types of savings accounts are closely convertible to currency, such as NOW accounts. The functionality and ease of conversion into currency governs the forms of money, which are defined differently. Sav-ings and loans, mutual savings, and similar institutions are not considered part of the commercial banking system and the currency and demand deposits of these institutions are not part of the M1 definition because these institutions are considered depository institutions. Other than tra-dition, it is not clear why savings accounts are not included in the defini-tion of M1. In the past, savings accounts were less accessible than checking account and also had a waiting time for withdrawals. Later, the waiting time was removed, especially for smaller amounts, but until all restrictions were removed in the 1980s, the procedure remained a two-step process. The two-step withdrawal process became almost automatic right before deregulation. When one wanted to withdraw money out of his/her savings account, the amount was deposited into his/her checking account and then was withdrawn from the checking account, thus requiring two signatures instead of one. In other words, M2 had to convert to M1 money before one received currency. After deregulation, one can withdraw from a savings account by writing a check, using a debit card, or stopping by an ATM. It is equally less clear why credit cards are not included in the definition of M1.

The M1 definition of money does not cover all assets that can be used as money, with somewhat less liquidity than currency, such as time depos-its or savings accounts. Even without the new kinds of savings accounts that allow direct payment for transactions, it is easy to convert deposits from savings accounts into currency. While in the past some *shoe leather* cost was involved, this is no longer true as a free phone call or an Internet transaction will take care of many of the necessary financial transactions.

A visit to any bank's web page reveals numerous types of checking and savings accounts, not to mention certificates of deposit (CD) and other types of accounts. Usually, the easier it is to convert money from an account to currency, the lower is the interest rate for the account, because less liquid accounts allow the bank enough time to acquire sufficient funds, to pay withdrawal requests, if necessary. The bank has to maintain higher amounts of cash to meet higher rates of withdrawals from accounts with lower interest rates, thus incur loss of revenue, which explains the lower interest rates for more liquid accounts, other things equal. Holding cash does not generate money for banks, but lending does. To reduce the chance that depositors would withdraw money from their accounts, the banks can use the law, as in the case of savings account, or contractual agreements, as in the case of CD. These certificates have a set period of maturity. A withdrawal before the maturity of CD would result in the loss of some or all the interest and even some penalty, depending on the specific terms of the contract. These reduce the incentive to withdraw and increase the portion of the deposit that the bank can lend. In return, the account receives a higher interest rate. Therefore, less liquid assets pay higher interest rates. Interest rates depend on many other factors, some of which will be explained in this manuscript. Assets can be ordered by their liquidity, as follows:

- Currency
- Demand deposits (checking accounts)
- Time deposits (savings accounts)
- Savings accounts at savings and loan institutions and mutual savings banks
- CD
- U.S. government savings bonds
- Marketable U.S. government securities

Broader, Less Liquid Money Definition

Until April 1971, the Federal Reserve Bank defined money only in terms of its most liquid form that met the purpose of acting as a *medium of exchange*, which is called the M1 money supply, as discussed previously. Nevertheless, other less liquid forms of money also serve the functions of money.

M2 consists of M1, in addition to the following: (1) savings deposits (including money market deposit accounts or MMDA);

(2) small-denomination time deposits (time deposits in amounts of less than $100,000), less individual retirement account (IRA) and Keogh balances at depository institutions; and (3) balances in retail money market mutual funds, less IRA and Keogh balances at money market mutual funds. Seasonally adjusted M2 is constructed by summing savings deposits, small-denomination time deposits, and retail money funds, each seasonally adjusted separately, and adding this result to seasonally adjusted M1.

M3 consists of M2 plus time deposits at mutual savings banks and savings and loan associations, and shares held at credit unions. It is worth mentioning that the data on deposits for the so-called thrift institutions are available only for the last day of the month, and to make them compatible with the customary definitions of M1 and M2, it is necessary to average them. The estimated averages are added to the monthly averages of M2.

M4 consists of M2 plus negotiable CDs over $100,000.
M5 consists of M3 plus negotiable CDs over $100,000.

The data on large denomination CDs are available on Wednesdays. It is necessary to average these weekly reports to obtain the average monthly data for M4 and M5. The definitions of different types of money have also been changing, making it difficult to compare different definitions with each other and with themselves over time. Bernanke, in comparing definitions of types of money between 1971 and 2006, claims that the 2006 definition of M1 is closer to its older definition, whereas the 2006 definition of M2 is equivalent to the 1971 definition of M3.[1] Additionally, the new definition of M3 is the same as that of the old M5. These and other changes made both M4 and M5 obsolete and they were discontinued after the 1989 re-definition of money types.

The M2 definition of money is also known as the Chicago Approach to money. Augmenting the definition of money from M1 to M2 provides a better explanation of the link between national income and money (M2), and validates the point of view of quantity theorists, such as Friedman, a long time professor at The University of Chicago. The *assets* included in different definitions of money are *substitutes* for each other and for currency. The only thing that is different among them is the degree of substitutability.

The Dollar as an International Currency

The U.S. dollar has been an international currency since at least the Bretton Woods Conference in 1944. In anticipation of victory, 44 allied nations met to decide the fate of international monetary and financial markets, international trade, and economic recovery. The results were several long-lasting institutions and the supremacy of the U.S. dollar. The conference resulted in the creation of the International Monetary Fund, the General Agreement on Tariffs and Trade (GATT), and the International Bank for Reconstruction and Development, which is now part of the World Bank. The GATT evolved through periodic meetings, mostly focused on tariffs and in 1995, it was completely replaced by the World Trade Organization. For the purposes of this book, the most relevant outcome of Bretton Woods is the supremacy of the U.S. dollar as the dominant international currency. It is estimated that between 50% and 75% of U.S. dollars are in circulation outside the United States. Consequently, it is more difficult to know exactly how much currency, which is part of the M1 money definition, is actually in the system. Because the velocity has always been considered the factor that balances the two sides of the equation of exchange, it is important to know the other components precisely.

The Supply of Money

This brief introduction is not meant to address all the nuances of the supply of money or to address the changes that are made to these definitions of money in order to keep them meaningful and useful. Anderson and Kavajecz provide a detailed trace of all changes to money, from M1 to M5 and all the related definitions such as M1A, M1B, and L.[2] A primary purpose of these definitions is to allow the Fed to determine the state of the economy and its need for money. Too much money in the system is inflationary, while too little will stifle economic activities and incomes. Over time, the rules and regulations that govern financial institutions shift in response to changes in economic conditions, technology, pressures from special interest groups, and the political and ideological orientations of leaders in different parts of the government and in industry. These changes affect what is considered money, and it is necessary to define money appropriately to determine the amount of money in the economy so that suitable monetary and fiscal policies can be implemented. With the exception of the M1 definition of money, the concept of money is not the same in all countries because of differences in the specific types of financial arrangements available to the financial institutions of different countries. However, one thing remains the same. All specific assets that are included in different definitions of money in different countries are all close substitutes for each other and currency, and only the liquidity of the assets differs. Some of the factors that affect the supply of money are not even a part of the definition of money. For example, on December 14, 1982, the Depository Institution Deregulation Committee (DIDC) revised Regulation Q to eliminate interest rate ceilings on MMDA with a required minimum balance of $2,500. On January 1, 1986, DIDC eliminated the interest rate ceilings on NOW accounts, as well as time deposits with less than thirty-one days. The changes to these regulations do not affect the content of a particular definition of money, but play a major role in how people handle their money. Because Regulation Q limits the maximum rate payable to time deposits by commercial bands, the amount of money in M2 is distorted when the interest rate gets close to or reaches the ceiling.[3] Consequently, it seems that the use of the M1 or M2 definition of money results in different estimates of the monetary impact of policy changes. In 1978, the Congress began the process of phasing out Regulation Q and replaced it with Section 204.10b of Regulation D.[4]

Table 6.1 provides the supply of money based on different definitions. Different assets, and hence, different definitions of money, are just substitutes for money is evident from the fact that individual definitions show more volatility than the aggregate supply of money. In other words, the overall money stock does not change as radically as the different forms of money that are defined more narrowly. The more rapid changes in narrower definitions of money indicate that over time different types of assets have been substituted for currency. These substitutions have been made possible by changes in regulations governing financial intermediaries that allow them to serve as money, but have other advantages, such as earning interest or being less subject to loss or theft. Table 6.1 includes seasonally adjusted and nonadjusted monthly data for ten years. The monthly data

Table 6.1. Supply of Money by Type of Money 1959–2012

Series description	Seasonally adjusted	Seasonally adjusted	Not adjusted	Not adjusted
unit	currency	currency	currency	currency
Multiplier:	1.00E + 09	1.00E + 09	1.00E + 09	1.00E + 09
Currency:	USD	USD	USD	USD
Period	M1.M	M2.M	M1_N.M	M2_N.M
2003–01	1,227.1	5,770.9	1,225.3	5,759.5
2003–02	1,238.0	5,807.8	1,225.2	5,787.0
2003–03	1,238.6	5,823.8	1,244.8	5,848.0
2003–04	1,250.3	5,867.2	1,259.3	5,904.4
2003–05	1,268.7	5,924.1	1,266.3	5,903.9
2003–06	1,280.0	5,959.5	1,284.4	5,958.2
2003–07	1,288.3	6,014.5	1,287.6	6,001.3
2003–08	1,294.5	6,058.7	1,291.9	6,057.9
2003–09	1,297.6	6,041.7	1,285.9	6,029.3
2003–10	1,297.3	6,030.2	1,288.5	6,014.1
2003–11	1,297.8	6,030.0	1,293.6	6,042.8
2003–12	1,306.6	6,036.8	1,332.2	6,064.2
2004–01	1,306.0	6,042.6	1,301.5	6,024.8
2004–02	1,320.7	6,078.5	1,306.3	6,055.4
2004–03	1,329.3	6,119.8	1,337.5	6,135.2
2004–04	1,333.2	6,161.5	1,342.8	6,202.7
2004–05	1,332.6	6,228.3	1,333.1	6,216.4
2004–06	1,342.2	6,239.9	1,347.4	6,239.4
2004–07	1,340.6	6,252.5	1,338.5	6,245.8
2004–08	1,353.2	6,273.9	1,352.2	6,267.6
2004–09	1,362.1	6,312.3	1,348.8	6,301.2
2004–10	1,360.7	6,335.5	1,351.0	6,323.1
2004–11	1,374.9	6,372.3	1,370.7	6,372.8
2004–12	1,375.9	6,388.5	1,401.2	6,415.2
2005–01	1,366.4	6,388.0	1,361.2	6,372.3
2005–02	1,371.6	6,403.3	1,354.7	6,373.2
2005–03	1,371.9	6,416.2	1,381.4	6,433.0

(*Continued*)

Table 6.1. Supply of Money by Type of Money 1959–2012
(Continued)

Series description	Seasonally adjusted	Seasonally adjusted	Not adjusted	Not adjusted
unit	currency	currency	currency	currency
Multiplier:	1.00E + 09	1.00E + 09	1.00E + 09	1.00E + 09
Currency:	USD	USD	USD	USD
Period	M1.M	M2.M	M1_N.M	M2_N.M
2005–04	1,358.2	6,424.4	1,369.0	6,476.5
2005–05	1,366.0	6,440.0	1,369.1	6,428.1
2005–06	1,379.2	6,476.0	1,384.0	6,480.3
2005–07	1,366.9	6,500.7	1,365.0	6,499.8
2005–08	1,377.2	6,534.4	1,376.5	6,523.6
2005–09	1,377.5	6,572.1	1,363.1	6,556.3
2005–10	1,375.4	6,602.6	1,364.9	6,583.3
2005–11	1,375.8	6,626.5	1,373.0	6,623.6
2005–12	1,374.7	6,654.6	1,396.6	6,676.1
2006–01	1,379.6	6,692.1	1,374.9	6,673.9
2006–02	1,379.1	6,720.1	1,361.5	6,691.5
2006–03	1,383.5	6,731.8	1,394.3	6,764.0
2006–04	1,380.9	6,764.7	1,393.2	6,827.2
2006–05	1,387.4	6,776.3	1,391.6	6,766.3
2006–06	1,373.6	6,814.0	1,378.6	6,819.6
2006–07	1,369.8	6,848.0	1,368.1	6,840.9
2006–08	1,371.7	6,878.3	1,370.1	6,859.2
2006–09	1,362.6	6,905.0	1,346.9	6,886.1
2006–10	1,370.2	6,960.1	1,359.8	6,928.6
2006–11	1,370.3	6,998.4	1,368.0	6,990.8
2006–12	1,366.3	7,038.4	1,387.1	7,065.3
2007–01	1,372.6	7,076.7	1,368.4	7,063.0
2007–02	1,364.0	7,096.7	1,346.9	7,074.8
2007–03	1,366.8	7,127.1	1,377.8	7,172.6
2007–04	1,378.1	7,195.8	1,391.8	7,262.6
2007–05	1,381.5	7,218.2	1,385.0	7,208.1

(Continued)

Table 6.1. Supply of Money by Type of Money 1959–2012 (Continued)

Series description	Seasonally adjusted	Seasonally adjusted	Not adjusted	Not adjusted
unit	currency	currency	currency	currency
Multiplier:	1.00E + 09	1.00E + 09	1.00E + 09	1.00E + 09
Currency:	USD	USD	USD	USD
Period	M1.M	M2.M	M1_N.M	M2_N.M
2007–06	1,365.2	7,242.1	1,370.2	7,252.0
2007–07	1,368.8	7,274.3	1,368.1	7,255.1
2007–08	1,375.0	7,338.4	1,372.2	7,315.4
2007–09	1,373.2	7,362.0	1,355.7	7,336.2
2007–10	1,379.7	7,388.0	1,368.8	7,346.6
2007–11	1,370.8	7,417.5	1,369.9	7,405.8
2007–12	1,374.1	7,448.4	1,394.2	7,474.5
2008–01	1,379.2	7,480.5	1,375.3	7,472.4
2008–02	1,381.3	7,566.4	1,365.3	7,554.8
2008–03	1,388.1	7,622.9	1,400.5	7,689.3
2008–04	1,392.5	7,674.1	1,406.0	7,738.2
2008–05	1,393.8	7,683.8	1,396.0	7,680.3
2008–06	1,401.0	7,693.2	1,406.8	7,703.0
2008–07	1,418.4	7,747.8	1,417.3	7,715.3
2008–08	1,404.8	7,737.1	1,400.9	7,713.2
2008–09	1,461.6	7,832.6	1,441.1	7,788.0
2008–10	1,474.1	7,941.1	1,462.2	7,896.7
2008–11	1,512.3	7,989.5	1,513.2	7,985.8
2008–12	1,604.7	8,183.2	1,631.8	8,204.8
2009–01	1,584.2	8,245.9	1,580.2	8,249.3
2009–02	1,568.4	8,283.9	1,551.4	8,277.4
2009–03	1,578.8	8,341.9	1,594.2	8,411.9
2009–04	1,612.3	8,344.4	1,626.9	8,411.2
2009–05	1,616.4	8,388.3	1,617.1	8,394.1
2009–06	1,656.2	8,407.7	1,661.0	8,407.1
2009–07	1,658.2	8,407.4	1,656.9	8,374.0

(Continued)

Table 6.1. Supply of Money by Type of Money 1959–2012
(Continued)

Series description	Seasonally adjusted	Seasonally adjusted	Not adjusted	Not adjusted
unit	currency	currency	currency	currency
Multiplier:	1.00E + 09	1.00E + 09	1.00E + 09	1.00E + 09
Currency:	USD	USD	USD	USD
Period	M1.M	M2.M	M1_N.M	M2_N.M
2009–08	1,657.2	8,388.4	1,650.5	8,353.4
2009–09	1,662.9	8,409.8	1,640.2	8,361.8
2009–10	1,678.3	8,441.0	1,663.5	8,394
2009–11	1,679.9	8,472.4	1,682.3	8,469.2
2009–12	1,695.4	8,486.6	1,723.6	8,511.4
2010–01	1,675.0	8,418.7	1,673.4	8,431.8
2010–02	1,701.5	8,482.5	1,684.4	8,475.7
2010–03	1,711.9	8,475.0	1,728.8	8,543.3
2010–04	1,700.0	8,502.4	1,715.2	8,568.2
2010–05	1,710.2	8,546.2	1,707.4	8,550.4
2010–06	1,728.0	8,570.4	1,731.6	8,572.5
2010–07	1,721.0	8,581.6	1,717.6	8,542.9
2010–08	1,746.7	8,623.4	1,738.8	8,573.7
2010–09	1,763.7	8,664.8	1,740.6	8,615.1
2010–10	1,780.1	8,710.3	1,766.6	8,675.6
2010–11	1,825.6	8,752.2	1,827.9	8,740.9
2010–12	1,836.3	8,781.8	1,870.5	8,822.6
2011–01	1,854.4	8,800.6	1,854.7	8,815.1
2011–02	1,876.0	8,856.8	1,857.8	8,852.7
2011–03	1,890.0	8,899.4	1,908.5	8,966.1
2011–04	1,902.1	8,947.6	1,917.0	9,021.1
2011–05	1,940.2	8,999.7	1,933.2	8,990.8
2011–06	1,951.9	9,080.1	1,953.2	9,079.2
2011–07	1,998.3	9,266.3	1,993.5	9,231.5
2011–08	2,112.0	9,489.6	2,100.8	9,425.8
2011–09	2,123.2	9,519.4	2,098.1	9,464.0

(Continued)

Table 6.1. Supply of Money by Type of Money 1959–2012 (Continued)

Series description	Seasonally adjusted	Seasonally adjusted	Not adjusted	Not adjusted
unit	currency	currency	currency	currency
Multiplier:	1.00E + 09	1.00E + 09	1.00E + 09	1.00E + 09
Currency:	USD	USD	USD	USD
Period	M1.M	M2.M	M1_N.M	M2_N.M
2011–10	2,141.8	9,549.0	2,127.1	9,513.3
2011–11	2,159.5	9,601.2	2,163.3	9,595.1
2011–12	2,160.4	9,637.1	2,206.9	9,690.0
2012–01	2,200.1	9,710.6	2,206.5	9,721.7
2012–02	2,215.0	9,745.9	2,191.9	9,746.8
2012–03	2,221.9	9,782.1	2,243.5	9,862.6
2012–04	2,250.8	9,825.5	2,265.9	9,907.1
2012–05	2,260.7	9,867.5	2,245.6	9,841.0
2012–06	2,265.4	9,918.6	2,263.3	9,918.8
2012–07	2,310.8	10,010.0	2,303.8	9,955.8
2012–08	2,339.0	10,082.4	2,325.7	10,018.4
2012–09	2,373.8	10,158.8	2,349.9	10,115.3
2012–10	2,419.5	10,242.7	2,406.8	10,193.4
2012–11	2,403.5	10,293.6	2,405.6	10,289.7
2012–12	2,440.2	10,402.4	2,497.9	10,475.7

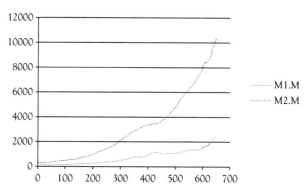

Figure 6.1. Seasonally adjusted monthly M1 and M2, 1959–2012.

are adjusted for seasonal fluctuation to provide a more realistic picture of the supply of money.

Figure 6.1 depicts historical seasonally adjusted monthly M1 and M2 data from 1959 to 2012, which is 658 months. Table 6.1 shows only part of the historical data, due to space constraints.

SECTION III

The Role of Interest Rate

CHAPTER 7

Rate of Return and Interest Rate

The Role of Interest Rate

One of the main shortcomings of the classical quantity theory is that it does not address the fact that the demand for money is affected by the interest rate. Recall from Chapter 1 that the equation of exchange is

$$MV = PQ \qquad (7.1)$$

According to the equation of exchange, the amount of money in the economy times its velocity equals the overall expenditures on all traded goods and services. This equation represents an inevitable reality and is, in fact, an identity, not an equation. An increase in economic activity—the right-hand side of the identity—would and should, inevitably, result in an equal increase on the left-hand side of the identity. Perhaps the biggest shortcoming of the equation of exchange is the fact that it does not address why or how the right-hand side of the equation changes. Another problem is that the relationship does not directly address the issue of demand for money. Classical economists simply stated that an increase in total economic activity necessitates an increase in the demand for money. As explained in Chapter 1, they extended the argument in the opposite direction, by stating that an increase in the supply of money has to be matched by an increase in the right-hand side of the identity. Because real output is a function of technology, employment, and capital, and as it cannot change due to changes in the money supply, the only way the right-hand side can increase is through inflation. History provides ample examples of inflation after increases in the supply of money. During the period of the classical economists, these increases were in the form of precious metals, and thus, subject to the discovery and mining of new sources for gold and silver.

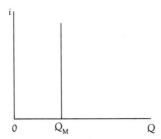

Figure 7.1. An inelastic demand for money.

As indicated in Chapter 2, there are at least three motives for demand for money, one of which is speculative motive. Demand for money due to speculative motive is based on the expectations of a return to holding an interest-bearing portfolio, such as stocks and bonds.

Changes in portfolio earnings change the rates of return, which in turn change the interest rate. Changes in the interest rate must change the demand for money; otherwise, the demand for money would be inelastic with respect to the interest rate.

An inelastic demand for money, which is implied by the quantity theory, does not accord with conventional demand theory, where the expected slope of the demand for a good is negative. Instead, an inelastic demand function is perpendicular to the quantity axis and parallel to the interest rate axis, as in Figure 7.1. Following the convention, the interest rate, represented by i, is on the vertical axis and the quantity demanded, represented by Q, is on the horizontal axis.

In addition to all the theoretical problems that a vertical demand function causes, it also fails to explain how the economy, or individuals, depending on whether the analysis is macro or micro, has reached the Q_M level in the first place. Under an infinitely inelastic demand function, the price of the good—which in this case is the interest rate—could be infinitely high or very low. In the case of inelastic demand the interest rate depends on the supply of money. Assuming an upward sloping supply function, as was true during the classical economists' era, the intersection of the supply and demand for money would determine the interest rate. Under a gold or silver currency regime in an era dominated by an insatiable demand for money, the production and cost of precious metals would increase without bound. In more recent times, during which the currency is not backed by precious metals and the cost of printing money is minimal, in comparison to the value of the note, a more realistic shape for the supply of money is vertical instead of upward sloping. The supply of money is determined by a government agency. In the case of the United States, that agency is the Federal Reserve Bank System. The Fed determines how much money should be in the economy, and thus, determines the supply of money, while the Bureau of Engraving and Printing of the Department of Treasury handles the actual printing.

What Is Interest Rate?

What is the interest rate and why is interest charged and paid? The notion of paying or receiving interest when borrowing or lending has been ingrained in Western culture to the point that most people accept it without questioning it or sometimes knowing what it really means or why it exists.

Every good and service, including money, provides utility. In order to gain this utility, we give up something to obtain the good or service. In modern economies, in almost all cases, the thing that is given up to obtain a good is money, as explained in Chapter 1. In the case of money, there is no other good to be exchanged. Note that if another good is given up in order to obtain money, the transaction is called a *sale*, which is not what we are addressing here. The only thing that is obtained in return for giving up money is more money, which is called *interest*. In this approach, we define the interest rate as follows:

Definition

The interest rate is the price of lending and borrowing money.

This definition is sufficient to explain the prevailing attitude toward money; namely, if you want (to borrow) some money, you must pay a price, which is the interest rate. This definition, however, does not explain why there should be an interest rate and begs an explanation. The definition provides an implicit reason for what might cause the interest rate to change. When the demand for loanable funds exceeds its supply, the interest rate will increase, while the interest rate will decrease when the supply of loanable funds exceeds its demand. However, the factors that cause changes in the demand and supply of loanable funds are unexplained by the provided explanation.

An assumption in economics is that consuming something desirable today is preferred to consuming it in the future. Recall that money is used to obtain other goods and services that provide direct utility. We are ignoring the possibility that holding money might provide direct utility to some people. If this assumption is correct, then the interest rate provides a measure of the difference in the utility of consuming a good today *versus* consuming it in the future, which would be the consequence of lending money instead of using it at the present time. Therefore, the lower utility of spending a given amount in the future, as compared to the present time, is one justification for charging interest on money for lending.

Borrowing *Versus* Owning Capital

Borrowing money gives one the advantage of being able to consume now instead of in the future. Based on the above discussion, the borrower should be willing to pay something extra, which is the interest, to consume immediately instead of in the future. Similar arguments can be made when money is used to invest in producing goods and services that could be sold for profit. Therefore, part of that return to investment can be, and in fact is, expected to be shared with the original owner of the capital. The difference between lending money and forming partnerships in investment is the form of risk. The risk of production is different than the risk of lending money. It seems reasonable to not only compensate the lender for postponing his consumption, thus incurring the loss of utility, but also to compensate him for the potential risk of losing all or part of the capital due to loan default. When a lending institution is calculating its interest rate, it has to take into account the reasonable amount that should be received due to delaying current consumption. In addition, it has to assess the probability of loan default. Finally, it has to pay for the cost of operating the business.

Part of the probability of default depends on the venture the borrower is pursuing. The probability of success in bread production is different than that of searching for sunken ship treasures under the seas. A person with an established income stream, a sound business plan, and a proven loan payment history would be subject to a much lower interest rate than someone lacking these characteristics. A lender would always lend his money to someone who has a lower risk, a better credit history, a higher revenue stream, and a better business plan, other things equal. Therefore, the marginal, or the last, person who is approved for a given sum of money is the one with the highest risk, the worst credit history, the lowest revenue stream, and the poorest business plan per period. After the more desirable borrowers receive their loans, the rest of the available funds are allocated to less desirable borrowers until all the funds are allocated. Credit rating companies provide ratings for potential borrowers based on their credit history, income, and assets among other things. These ratings provide a reference for determining the appropriate interest rate to charge. On the borrower side, the lender with the lowest rate and most appealing terms are depleted before the less desirable lenders are approached. The process continues until the amount borrowed at a given rate of interest, plus all the applicable surcharges, equals the amount of the capital that will be diverted to present consumption rather than future consumption.

In summary, the lenders pick the most appealing borrowers and the borrowers pick the most appealing lenders first. The process continues until all the loanable funds and all the borrowers' needs are met. The interest rate that equalizes the two sides is the market clearing interest rate. The market clearing interest rate is the rate without the premium for extra risk of the risky borrowers, and is therefore, the lowest interest rate for the most favorable borrower. For this reason it is called the *benchmark* interest rate. In the United States, the benchmark interest rate is closely related to the Federal funds rate. The rates of the official banks of other countries are also used as a benchmark rate.

What Determines the Interest Rate That Borrowers Are Willing to Pay?

The variables that affect the willingness and ability to pay a particular rate of interest depend on several factors. The most important distinguishing factor is the purpose of the loan. There is a distinct difference between borrowing for consumption and borrowing for investment. When borrowing for consumption, the utility of present consumption *versus* the utility of future consumption determines the amount the borrower is willing to pay for the loan. This depends on individual taste and preferences. The people for whom the utility loss due to payment of the market interest rate is less than the difference in utility of consuming now *versus* in the future would borrow, while others would not. A similar analogy applies to individual lenders, or savers, who will lend their money, as long as the utility of receiving the market interest rate is higher than the loss of utility of postponing their consumption.

When funds are borrowed for investment purposes, the borrower does not receive any utility because he or she is not consuming anything. The factor that affects the ability to borrow is the return to investment, known as the *internal rate of return*.

Internal Rate of Return

In order to comprehend the concept of an internal rate of return, or the marginal efficiency of investment, it is necessary to define the concept of the *discounted present value*. The discounted present value converts streams of future earnings into their value at the present time. Suppose there are two streams of revenue possibility over the next three years. One yields $100 at the end of each year for total yield of $300 above the original capital. The other one yields $50, $150, and $100 at the end of each of the three years, respectively, for the same total yield of $300 above the original capital. A mathematical procedure converts all the future income into their present value, which identifies which one has higher present value.

Definition

The present value of future income is the amount of money that, if lent at the current interest rate, would result in the same amount of income in the future as the income that was targeted.

Here we will not prove the mathematical steps. Let P_0 represent the present value of a single income in the future, P_1, where i is the interest rate.

$$P_0 = \frac{1}{1+i} P_1 \qquad (7.2)$$

P_0 is the discounted present value of one-period-ahead income of P_1. For convenience, we can represent

$$\frac{1}{1+i} = D \qquad (7.3)$$

D is called the *discount factor*. The relationship for a single sum of P_2 amount for n years in the future is calculated as follows:

$$P_0 = D^n P_2 \qquad (7.4)$$

The more general case of receiving different sums in different years is represented by

$$S_n = \frac{1 - D^{n+1}}{1 - D} \qquad (7.5)$$

where S is the sum of the discounted present value of streams of identical income in every period for n periods. If n is indefinite, as in the case of perpetuity bond, the formula becomes

$$S_n = \frac{1}{1 - D} \qquad (7.6)$$

When the streams of future incomes are different, as in the original example above, the present value of each future income is calculated and added up to get the total discounted present value of all future incomes.

Definition

The internal rate of return of an investment is the rate of interest that would equate the discounted present value of the expected future yields to the cost of investment.

Care must be taken to assure that only the additional yields are used and not the cumulative yields. Because the additional values are known as *marginal values* in economics, the internal rate of return is also known as the *marginal efficiency of investment*.

The same principle applies when the stream of earnings is from an investment instead of borrowing, except it is called the *internal rate of return*. While calculating the discounted future earnings, the discounted future operation and maintenance costs are also considered.

Definition

The internal rate of return evaluates the internal profitability of an investment.

A firm will invest if its internal rate of return exceeds the interest rate. Figure 7.2 depicts the relationship between the discounted present value, on the vertical axis, and the discounted interest rate, on the horizontal axis. In the figure, the firm will invest if the point where the curve intersects the horizontal axis, point E, is to the right of point C for the project.

In Figure 7.2, the marginal efficiency of investment is the interest rate *C* on the intersection point of the curve and the horizontal axis. Because investment projects will be undertaken until the marginal efficiency of investment equals the projects' present value cost, their difference will be zero, and hence, the curve intersects the horizontal axis. The firm knows

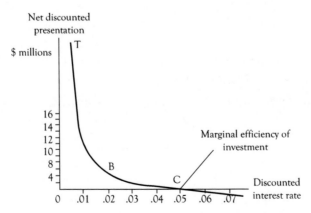

Figure 7.2. Discounted present value versus discounted interest rate.

the market interest rate, point B, which in this example is 2%. At this rate, the net discounted present value of the investment is $4 million. The curve T has a negative slope because an increase in the discounted interest rate reduces the present value of investment.

Market Interest Rate

At any given time there is a certain amount of loanable funds for each interest rate. The higher the interest rate, other things equal, the greater the amount of loanable funds will be. Similarly, for every level of interest rate, there is a demand for loans. The higher the interest rate, other things equal, the less the demand for loans will be. The intersection of the market demand and supply of loanable funds determines the market clearing interest rate. The supply and demand for loans are determined and influenced by each of the factors discussed previously.

CHAPTER 8

Determining
the Interest Rate

Capital Budgeting and the Interest Rate

The interest rate plays an important role in investment decisions. An entrepreneur needs capital to invest. The process of making investment decisions is known as *capital budgeting*. Capital budgeting is a complex process and involves numerous stages such as choosing appropriate products in which to invest in each period, choosing when to introduce the product to the market, deciding how much to produce, determining how capital should be allotted, identifying necessary sources of loanable funds, and creating a business plan for the project. These and other related materials are discussed in the theory of capital, the details of which are beyond the scope of this text.

Some of the factors affecting capital budgeting are difficult to manage. Imperfect information, inability to forecast risk, uncertainty, variation in people's tastes and preferences, and changing economic conditions make capital budgeting difficult. Many of these factors are not controlled by the entrepreneur, and there are no reliable methods of providing a reasonable forecast for these factors either. There are some theories based on statistical analysis that address probabilistic outcomes, but they are more suitable for an advanced text on the topic. In real life, businesspersons have to make decisions without being able to forecast risk, uncertainty, or the other factors listed. Some get lucky and succeed, while others fail. This unknown and uncertain risk must also be incorporated into projections of the return of loanable funds. Bankers use the risk-adjusted return on capital for making decisions about loans.

It is important to point out that in economics the terms *investment* and *capital* are not used to indicate the acquisition of stocks and bonds, or holding them. The term *capital* refers to *real* assets, such as factories, raw materials, machinery, and inventory of goods, either in the process of production or finished. One can distinguish between physical capital and financial capital, as stock or flow. Marx used physical and financial *capital* in a combined sense, both of which belong to the capitalist, as does the resulting flow of income. Capital is anything that is produced for the purpose of producing other goods rather than for final consumption. The production or acquisition of real capital assets is *investment*. Investment is the difference between capital assets in two adjacent periods.

To invest, a firm may use own funds or borrow. The colloquial *capital* usually refers to loanable funds, deposits in the bank, or cash. Placing one's money in a savings account, purchasing stocks or bonds, or buying an existing home does not constitute investment in an economic sense. These behaviors represent different kinds of saving, and because saving is a type of consumption in economic analysis, all of these activities are a form of consumption. Although the purchase of an existing home is a form of consumption, the construction of a new home is considered an investment.

Economic Profit *Versus* Accounting Profit

It is worthwhile to clarify another misused term, *profit*. It is customary to refer to the return on any investment as profit. Part of the return to investment is the interest for the capital and another part is usually the return to entrepreneur, which should be regarded as labor cost. To employ labor and capital, the prevailing wage and interest rate must be paid, regardless of who owns the labor or the capital. When an entrepreneur utilizes his/her own labor and capital, part of the earnings of the enterprise are compensations for those components and cannot be considered profit. Public corporations hire capital and managers and have to pay for them. Under perfect competition, the price of goods and services will be sufficient to pay for the fair market value of capital and labor and nothing is left. In market structures other than perfect competition and occasionally when there is disequilibrium in the market under perfect competition, it is possible to earn more than the fair values of capital and labor, which is called *economic profit*.

Definition

Perfect competition is a market structure in which there are many buyers and sellers of a good or a service, there is perfect and complete information available to all the parties, there is free entry and exit for buyers and sellers, and the individual goods are not distinguishable from each other.

There is hardly any product in the twenty-first century in an industrialized country that is exchanged in a perfectly competitive market. In a perfectly competitive market, economic profit can exist only in the short run and when the market is shifting from one long-run equilibrium to another long-run equilibrium due to temporary market imperfections. Consider an occasion in a perfectly competitive market where there is an economic profit in the short run, that is, the revenue exceeds the cost after all the factors of production are paid, regardless of who owns them.

Therefore, the firm is receiving a premium over all the other firms in the market. The excess revenue in the production of the good in this firm will attract producers from other sectors of the economy, provided those sectors have free entry and exit as well. The increase in the number of producers in the market has two effects. First, the supply increases, thus the price decreases. Second, the production cost increases due to higher demand, by the new entrants, for the resources used in the market thus increasing their costs. The increase in the cost and the decrease in the revenue eliminate the short-run economic profit of the firm. Therefore, in perfectly competitive markets, the *economic profit is zero* when the economy is in equilibrium. In the long run, firms will move in and out of particular productions, and hence, the economy will be at an equilibrium point.

The Discount Rate and Interest Rate

In Chapter 7, we introduced the concept of the discount rate. The discount rate is the opportunity cost of receiving money in the future instead of now. In a perfect money market, any funds received now, P, can be utilized to receive iP in one year, where i is the interest rate. The opportunity cost of receiving funds in one year instead of now is iP. In one year, the total value of receiving $\$P$ today is $P + iP = (1 + i)P$. Therefore, the present value of $\$(1 + i)P$ in one year is $\$P$. Because multiplying $(1 + i)P$

by $1/(1 + i)$ results in P, the ratio $1/(1 + i)$ is the *discount rate*. Having $\$P$ today is the same as having $\$(1 + i)P$ in one year. Therefore, the opportunity cost of not receiving $\$P$ is $\$iP$. The relationship between the interest rate and the discount rate is clear under a perfect money market; the discount rate is $1/(1 + i)$, and has an inverse relationship with the interest rate. An increase in the interest rate would decrease the discount rate, although in a nonlinear fashion. Every investment can potentially have a negative net discounted present value, depending on the interest rate.

The relationship between the interest rate and the discount rates is more complex when the money market is less than perfect. Recall that the money market is commonly called the capital market. Money market imperfections can manifest in several ways such as the existence of a limit on borrowing or the existence of an interest rate, which is lower than for borrowing for lending. Nevertheless, the discount rate is still the opportunity cost of delayed payment. Another money market imperfection can be demonstrated through the following example. Assume that an investment requires $40 million, the interest rate is 2%, and the expected rate of return on the investment is 8%. However, the entrepreneur can only borrow $30 million, and hence, is unable to undertake the investment. The opportunity cost in this case is 8%.

The functional form of the net discounted present value does not have to be downward sloping. It can have both positive and negative slopes depending on the interest rate and the expected return on investment. The larger the interest rate, the less significant a given earnings in the future, regardless of whether it is positive or negative. In such cases, the curve would oscillate around the horizontal axis as depicted in Figure 8.1.

Another complexity arises when there are two mutually exclusive investment opportunities in which the net discounted present values for the two intersect at least in one point. Consequently, one investment would be better before the intersection point, and the other one would be preferred after the intersection. The curve that is further from the origin is preferred over the segment to the right of the intersection (Figure 8.2).

When the firm is limited on the amount of loanable funds it can receive, there is no single logical decision that can be based on the interest rate. Therefore, whichever loan ends up being used for the investment, if any at all, will not result in the optimal choice. The interest rate associated

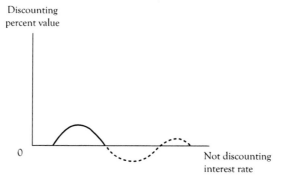

Figure 8.1. An example of a negative discounting interest rate.

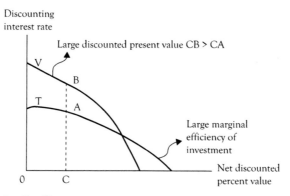

Figure 8.2. Conflicting investment opportunities.

with that loan, therefore, would not reflect the real opportunity cost of the funds to the firm and cannot be used to obtain the net discounted present value of the investment. The fact that there is no interest rate that can be used to calculate the net discounted present value when there is a limit on the amount of borrowing, and the interest rates for the alternative funding options are different does not preclude the ability to determine the appropriate investment for the firm. This process, however, is beyond the scope of this text and belongs in a text on capital budgeting.

Notwithstanding the few cases where the interest rate cannot be effectively used to calculate the net discounted present value, the interest rate that would make an investment a wise choice is obtained by the rule discussed at the beginning of the chapter. This rate is either higher or lower than the market interest rate. Assuming that the loanable funds market is not at equilibrium and there are loanable funds available if the rate is lower than the market rate, the firm will not invest. Consequently, the excess supply of loanable funds will drive the interest rates down, making more investments profitable, until all the available funds are equal to the needed funds at the prevailing interest rate. When the rate of interest that would make an investment a reasonable decision is higher than the one prevailing in the market, the firm will invest, and hence, reduce uncommitted loanable funds, thus, increasing the interest rate. This process will continue until all the loanable funds have been allocated to the firms that find investment profitable at the prevailing market interest rate. The rate at which the market is in equilibrium as a result of the above process is the point where the supply of loanable funds intersects the demand for loanable funds.

We briefly explained the capital market mechanism that determines the interest rate. However, earlier in the chapter, we pointed out that funds could also be borrowed for consumption purposes. Usually, the loans for small consumer goods are shorter in their terms to maturity than those for larger ones. It is not realistic to borrow/lend $50,000 to buy food or help with the rent. The relatively small amounts for such necessities of life are usually for less than a month or even shorter terms. Loans to obtain an education, buy a car, or purchase a home are much larger in magnitude and are usually for longer terms. The customary loan period for homes in the United States is thirty years. In the late twentieth century, when housing prices soared, forty year loans appeared in the market. Up until the mid-1990s, the terms for borrowing to purchase a car were thirty-six to forty-eight months, but with more expensive cars, the customary loan periods have increased to sixty to seventy-two months. Forty-year mortgages are customary in many countries. The microeconomic theories of consumption and utility that would explain how the borrowers decide on the appropriate amount to borrow and at what interest rate is a discussion better left for a microeconomics textbook. The lenders decision process to determine the interest rate for the purpose of lending for consumption instead of investment is similar. When borrowing for consumption, there is no expected income or return, so it does not make sense to require a business plan or feasibility study. When lending funds for consumption, the income and loan history of the borrower play the largest role in the decision to approve the loan. Although the process to determine the amount to borrow for consumption is different than the process for borrowing for investment, the sum of all such borrowings constitutes the demand for loanable funds. The intersection of the demand for and supply of loanable funds for consumption determines the market clearing interest rate. Because the supply of loanable funds for consumption or investment need not have the same slope, these are addressed separately. This same logic is behind separating the demand for loanable funds. Nevertheless, there is only one prevailing interest rate in the market as a whole; otherwise, the funds will move from loans for consumption to loans for investment or *vice versa*, until the interest rates are equalized.

Real *Versus* Nominal Interest Rates

The interest paid and received for loanable funds is based on the benefit that accrues to the borrower and the loss that ensues for the lender. All prices increase during inflation, including the price of money, which is the interest rate. It makes sense to adjust the interest rate, determined by the aforementioned mechanism, to include any price increases. Assume the market clearing interest rate is 4% and the inflation rate is 3%. In order to allow lenders to receive a 4% *real* return on their money, the *nominal* interest rate must be 4 + 3 = 7%. The value of a dollar today, when these are the prevailing rates, is equal to $1.07 in one year, of which, $1.00 is the original sum, 4 cents is the return to loanable fund, and the remaining 3 cents is the adjustment for inflation. The observed market interest rate always includes adjustments for the rate of inflation. This rate is known as the *nominal interest rate.* Dividing the nominal interest rate by the inflation rate yields the *real interest rate.*

The focus of economic analysis is the real interest rate. Money market transactions are based on the nominal interest rate. This increases the uncertainty of economic activities. In addition to all the computation necessary to determine whether a project is worth undertaking and borrowing funds for, businesspersons have to forecast the inflation rate for all the years for which capital budgeting is performed. A more pragmatic approach is to base economic decisions on the real interest rate with a built-in adjustment for inflation. A built-in inflation adjustment reduces forecast errors and results in a more efficient economy. The consequence of having to estimate and forecast the inflation rate is that it allows for speculation. The people who are able to forecast the inflation rate better will gain and the others will lose. Some people, even those with poor or no forecasting capabilities, guess what future inflation will be and use it in their decisions. Those who guess the future inflation rates more closely will gain and the rest will lose.

CHAPTER 9

The Role of Risk on the Interest Rate

Introduction

In the previous two chapters we referred to risk and how interest rates must be adjusted to reflect the risk associated with different ventures, as well as the borrowers' risks. Many important issues about risk were not discussed. What risk is, how it is calculated, and how it affects interest rates are some of the more obvious questions that were left unanswered.

The difference between risk and uncertainty is that the former has a possible undesirable consequence. The lower the probability, the less the chance of occurrence of the outcome, while the higher the probability, the greater the chance of occurrence. The smallest probability of occurrence is zero, while the largest is one. In the case of the latter, the outcome is certain, while in the case of the former, it is an impossible event. In the business world, the negative outcomes are reflected in low or no return, loss of initial investment capital, and similar financial calamities. Therefore, the discussion of risk hinges on the knowledge of probability and theories that govern it.

Uncertainty is often mistaken for risk. Part of the confusion is that both involve probability. The outcome of flipping a coin is uncertain, although the probability of observing a head or tail on a fair coin is 50%. Statistically speaking, the expected outcome of a head or a tail is 50%. Notice there is not any risk, although the outcome is uncertain. Running a red light or driving under the influence of alcohol could result in an accident, and shaking hands with a person infected with the flu could cause sickness. Each of these examples has a probable, yet undesirable outcome, and are, therefore, risky. In the business world, the outcome of a new investment is uncertain. The success of the venture depends on the desirability of the good produced and the cost of its production. The cost and revenue are functions of economic conditions that are unknown at the time of investment. The probability of some uncertain outcomes can be calculated.

Unfortunately, not everyone knows how to calculate probabilities, and even those who do, have difficulty assigning probability to risks for different financial endeavors. At first, it might seem to be impossible to assign probabilities to outcomes of financial decisions, especially when they depend on the behavior of individual people with diverse interests, utilities, preferences, and tastes. The probability of the risk of default on an investment in a new product depends on the usefulness of the product, the desire of people to buy it, the ability of consumers to afford it, and on continued use of the product. None of these are known for most existing products, let alone for a new product. However, there have been some basic methods used for incorporating risk into capital budgeting analysis. They are discussed here briefly.

Discounting for Risk

Chapter 8 demonstrated how the present values of future earnings make them comparable with the earnings at the present time, which makes it possible to know which future stream of income is higher. Similarly, future risks can be discounted to obtain their present time equivalent risk. The risk factor, σ, pronounced sigma, is treated similar to the interest rate, and the net discounted present value formula is augmented by including the risk for the case of one period ahead.

$$D = \frac{1}{1+i+\sigma} \qquad (9.1)$$

We purposefully use the lower-case Greek letter sigma, σ, because it is used to represent the standard deviation in statistics. The concept of standard deviation in statistics is synonymous with the concept of risk in economics and finance. Let us first provide a definition for standard deviation.

Definition

Standard deviation is the square root of variance and represents the average error of a variable.

Definition

Variance is the sum of the squares of the deviations of values from their mean, divided by population size. It is the average of the squared individual errors.[1]

The expected value of an outcome is the best estimate of what is expected to happen. When the expected outcome does not occur, the difference between the actual outcome and the expected outcome is called an *individual error*. The average of all such errors is, in a sense, the average riskiness of the outcome, which is also the standard deviation of the outcome.[1]

As before, the discounted present value formula is raised to the power *n* if the outcome is *n* periods in the future. Because both the risk and interest rate are non-negative values, the denominator is always larger than the numerator, implying that *D* is always less than one, but still positive. Raising a non-negative value that is less than one to powers higher than one reduces the magnitude of the number. Therefore,

$$D^n < D \quad \text{for} \quad n > 1$$

This makes perfect economic sense. The impact of risk in a distant future is less than the impact of the same level of risk in the near future. This is analogous to future income. The same level of earnings in the distant future is less valuable than in the near future, which in turn is less valuable than the present.

However, this analysis suffers from two problems. First, it does not indicate how the future risks are calculated. Second, it does not reflect people's attitude toward risk. Although the word *risk* refers to unexpected negative outcomes, there is no reason why someone should not value the thrill of a risk. After all, many people gamble at casinos knowing that the expected value of the game is negative, which means that on the average, gamblers lose. Their loss pays for the salaries and other expenses of operating a casino. People who are risk lovers receive utility from engaging in risky behavior, including risky business endeavors. These people would accept lower return for their investment because of the additional utility they receive from taking risk. The accepted assumption in economics is that (at least the majority of) people are *risk averse*. This assumption makes it easier to formulate economic theory, but does not solve all the problems. People can be risk averse to different extents. In practice, the issue of the extent of risk averseness of people is ignored. This allowed earlier works on risk to be based on a judgment call. An entrepreneur would be asked to give an estimated risk of a particular venture, which is used in the formula to obtain the net discounted present value of the investment.

This procedure was arbitrary at best and flawed at worst. For a market-level risk adjustment, massive data on identical investments is necessary, which are generally not available. The one exception is the selection of bundles of stocks and bonds, which are commonly known as a portfolio.

Applying the Probability Theory

Markowitz provides a procedure for the selection of a risky portfolio, which is calculable for widely traded stocks and bonds.[2] Markowitz introduces two indices, one for expected earnings and the other for risk. Note how the probability theory was being incorporated in the concept of expected earnings. Less obvious is the use of probability in finding the risk associated with different portfolio investments. Data availability enables the use of statistical procedures to estimate expected future earnings, thus solving one of the problems. The same data can be used to obtain the standard deviation, and hence, establish risk, albeit, historical risk. When economic conditions, expectations, and their observed trends remain the same, historical risk would be a reasonable estimate of future risk, thus solving the second problem. Risk-averse people demand higher returns for lending to offset higher risks. Therefore, one can establish pairs of risk-earning combinations that are plausible, as in curve PP in Figure 9.1, which is known as a *risk-earnings possibility curve*.

To complete the analysis, the concept of indifference curves from utility theory is combined with the risk-earnings possibility. Imagine a risk-earnings indifference curve in which the investor is indifferent between different earnings with different risk levels. Remember, that as risk increases, earnings must also increase to compensate for the increased risk. Two such indifference curves are included in Figure 9.1. These indifference curves would look strange to someone who is used to indifference

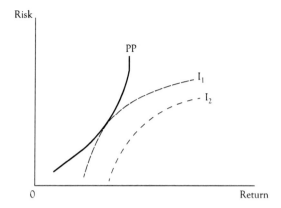

Figure 9.1. Risk-earnings possibility curve and indifference curves.

curves in utility theory. The reason is the orientation of the graph. We deliberately made the graph in such a way that earnings increase as the distance from the origin or the risk increases. Consequently, the indifference curves seem to be strange. A ninety-degree rotation to the left would make the indifference curves look normal. In either orientation, the graph is correct. As in the utility theory and production theory, the point of tangency between the risk-earnings possibility curve and risk-earnings indifference curve must be the correct point for the risk-earnings combination that maximizes consumers' earnings adjusted for risk. One of the advantages of the Markowitz procedure is that it predicts a diversified portfolio, which makes economic sense and reflects the actual behavior of the majority of investors.

Sensitivity Analysis

In management science, it is important to identify different sources of uncertainty and measure the contribution of each to the overall level of uncertainty. At the same time, it is important to determine which variables are crucial in making investment decisions. The present values of the outcomes are computed and their robustness is examined in response to changes in the identified crucial or strategic variables.

Those familiar with regression analysis will recognize the similarities between the two methods. The critical values are actually the independent variables and the object of the analysis is the dependent variable. In sensitivity analysis, the values of one or more variables are changed and the estimated values of the dependent variable are examined for unexpected outcomes and robustness. Those with management backgrounds will recognize the similarity with the *what-if* method that was widely in use during the 1990s. In the what-if analysis, a relationship between a desired outcome and factors that influence it is set up in a spreadsheet. After examining the outcome using simple values that would make it easier to verify the correctness of the outcome, the system is utilized by inserting expected or desired values for the factor and the outcome is assessed on whether it is acceptable or not. The what-if analysis is a crude version of regression, lacking theory, statistical rigor, or theoretical foundation. It is based on the experience of the people that set it up.

In sensitivity analysis, the dependent variable is the outcome of investment. Although techniques, such as *logit* and *probit* regressions, allow a dichotomous dependent variable, such as success or failure, it is more informative if the outcome is quantitative in nature, such as the return on investment, gross revenue, and the like. The crucial variables in the sensitivity analysis include all the variables with an uncertain outcome, such as the price of a crucial raw material (e.g. oil, copper or iron), future tax and inflation rates, regulations (e.g. clean air requirements), and a host of other variables whose future values are unknown. For example, let the success of an investment hinge on oil prices being under $110 per barrel for two years; this critical value, together with alternative prices for the product, is used to determine what price would be necessary to remain profitable if the price of oil exceeds $110. Then a value judgment is made on whether that price is feasible considering the expected inflation rate, price of competitors, and tax rates that would be in effect during the crucial first two years of the product. These few variables are addressed here to clarify the process. In practice, the list of variables is much longer. As the value of the critical variables is changed to reflect possible future values, we can modify the other variables to result in a specific output, such as a given level of earning or rate of return. A commonly used alternative is the point where the cost is equal to the revenue or the *break-even* point. When this approach is applied to the interest rate, the break-even point is where the net present value of an investment is zero.

The main shortcoming of sensitivity analysis is its ad hoc nature. All uncertain future values are guessed rather than estimated using statistical analysis. However, managers like this method because of its flexibility in considering numerous scenarios and its ability to allow decision makers to contemplate different outcomes, which they might believe to be plausible. It also enables them to explore cases of extreme possibilities or to forecast without data.

Decision Theory

In 1944, Neumann and Morgenstern introduced a new concept of rationality.[3] Their utility function indicates that a rational person has a utility function such that the expected utility can be maximized. The expected utility does not necessarily coincide with the mathematically expected value. The mathematical expected value would indicate that if an investment costs $3,000 and there is a 30% chance of earning $12,000, there is a 70% chance of earning zero dollars. The mathematical expected value of the investment is obtained by:

$$E(\text{earning}) = 30\% \ (12,000) + 70\% \ (0) = \$3,600$$

Because $3,600 is greater than $3,000, the investment is worthwhile. The example implicitly assumes that the earnings are instantaneous, something like gambling. Adding delay in earning necessitates application of the discount rate to obtain the present value of the earnings for the sake of comparison. However, this is a minor thing and a matter of computation. After choosing appropriate success rates and anticipated earnings, one can reach a conclusion on whether an investment would be profitable. Anytime the net discounted expected earnings exceed the cost, the investment is worthwhile. However, many people may not want to risk their last $3,000 in such a venture if they cannot afford zero earnings. The Neumann–Morgenstern rationality allows for the possibility of the latter decision because

Utility of $1 + Utility of $1 is not necessarily equal to the Utility of $2

When a person is rational under the Neumann–Morgenstern condition, he is maximizing his utility, not his expected value, as indicated by statistics. This utility maximizing procedure is the foundation of the decision theory, which has gained a respectable place in both management science and economics. Another application of their concept of rationality can be found in the economic game theory, which was later advanced by Nash.[4,5] Like many other topics in science, an earlier version of this concept was used in the discussion of oligopoly market structures.[6]

SECTION IV

Financial Systems

CHAPTER 10

Components of the Financial System

Introduction

The financial system is a collection of numerous and diverse groups of institutions that are engaged in financial transactions, both domestically and internationally. Banks are a major component of the financial system. Another major component of the system, the Federal Reserve Bank, was discussed extensively in Chapter 5. Other players in the system are mutual funds, investment banks, insurance companies, and finance companies. All of the institutions that deal with money and finance are, to some extent, regulated by the government. The degree of regulation and the resulting requirements differ from one group to another, as well as from one country to country. Regulations in different countries are the result of both historical developments and the need to meet specific expectations of different groups in each country. They facilitate the roles of the institutions in the overall financial market of the country. International transactions and financial interactions have necessitated the development of rules and regulations to protect the interests of different countries and to ensure dependable international operations.

In Chapters 1 and 2, we discussed how the use of money improves market transactions. Financial institutions play a similar role in the economy, especially the financial market. Suppose an individual has loanable funds and another person needs to borrow funds. Even in the information-filled twenty-first century, it is difficult for these two people to find each other. It is necessary to be able to trust the other party before engaging in a financial transaction. Usually, individuals are ill prepared to determine the risk of lending to strangers. There is also no assurance that the amount of one's loanable funds is exactly the same as the borrower's demand. Imagine having to borrow from several people with different interest rates, maturity dates, and payment schedules. Even if this was plausible, the borrower would end up paying several notes per period, which is a financial burden. Finally, the cost of keeping track of all these transactions for a single loan would be too high. These problems are similar to the barter dilemmas discussed in the introduction of this book. As in the case of barter, an institution is needed to facilitate transactions. In the financial markets these institutions are known as *financial intermediaries*. Regulations protect financial intermediaries from each other, as well as providing safeguards for borrowers and lenders. Similarly, regulations help the institutions to collect the funds they lend in case of default. As a result of facilitating transactions and reducing many of the problems of financial transactions, the financial intermediaries collect a fee, commensurate with the difficulty of the task, the amount of money involved, risk levels, and the duration of the financial contract. Financial intermediaries are for-profit enterprises; therefore, they are constantly finding new ways to make more profit. Financial products and services are known as *financial innovation*.

The Financial System

The financial system is a collection of institutions that facilitate financial transactions by collecting loanable funds from lenders and lending them to borrowers or facilitating financial transactions. Businesses use financial intermediaries to pay for new investments. A business can borrow funds for new investments, which is known as *debt*. Debts must be paid at predetermined intervals and specific amounts of principal and interest per period. Numerous contractual agreements are available from *interest-only* periodic payments (with a lump sum payment of principal at the end of the loan period) to fixed periodic payments, which means the majority of the fixed payment is interest payment at first, but the share of principal out of the fixed payments increases over time until the majority of the fixed payment consists of principal. Debt instruments are grouped by the length of expiration as short term (less than one year), intermediate term (between one and ten years), and long term (ten or more years). Government bonds, student loans, and corporate bonds are examples of debt instruments.

In this type of funding, the borrower takes the entire risk of running a business. The lender and borrower know exactly how much will be paid at the end of each period. The risk to the lender is limited to the risk of the borrower but not the risk of business. The lender's revenue stream is independent of the performance of the borrower's investment. Intermediate- and long-term debt instruments are traded in *capital markets*, while short-term debt instruments are exchanged in *money markets*. Money and capital market instruments will be discussed in more detail shortly. The information, liquidity, and risk associated with the money market are different than that of the capital market. The price fluctuations of short-term instruments are less than that of intermediate- and long-term debt instruments traded in the capital market. Money market instruments are also more liquid than capital market instruments and information is less costly for money market instruments than for capital market instruments. These factors impact lenders' and borrowers' decisions when choosing a market and an instrument.

The other type of arrangement for businesses is to obtain funds by selling a part of the ownership of the business. Thus, the investor obtains an *equity* share. Equity entitles the holder to a share of profits, which means the investor is actually taking the same risk as the borrower in the success of the business. Equity owners also own a share of the assets of the business, which is equal to their share. The common stock is an example of an equity instrument. In this type of funding, the lender's income stream fluctuates with the performance of the borrower's business. Neither party knows the exact amount of payment, known as dividend, until the end of the period when the firm's profit is determined.

Financial intermediaries function in *financial markets*. This is where lenders *meet* borrowers. When a lender buys equity shares of a company, the transaction is known as *direct finance*, which takes place in a primary market. A market is called a *primary market* when a newly issued equity is sold to an initial buyer. Governments use primary markets to finance major projects or to cover budget deficits. The market for trading the existing shares is called the *secondary financial markets*. There are several ways to trade assets in the secondary markets. In an *auction market*, the buyers and sellers bid for shares until a market clearing price is obtained. Usually, professional traders represent individual buyers and sellers that are not present at the market. The New York Stock Exchange is a well-known example of this type of market. Auction markets are called *exchanges*. In contrast to exchanges, *over-the-counter* markets do not have a centralized location for exchange. Dealers post buying or selling prices and transact with anyone who is willing to trade at their specific price. The use of computers and the Internet has facilitated the growth of such markets. By tradition, the equities of well known or large corporations are traded in the exchanges, while the shares of smaller or less known firms and U.S. government securities are exchanged in the over-the-counter markets.

Markets are categorized by the form of the trade. When the actual claim, or equity share, is bought or sold with immediate settlement, it is known as a cash market. When the settlement occurs at a time later than the time of transaction it is known as a *derivative market*. In a broader sense, derivatives can include futures and options. Derivative markets might help reduce transaction risk. The value of a derivative is derived from the asset it represents, such as bonds, stocks, or foreign exchanges. Sometimes, in addition to obtaining possession of the financial instrument in the future, the entire transaction can be finalized in the future as well, the price of which will be determined at the time of settlement. This transaction is called *financial futures*. When instead of the time, the price is predetermined in the financial future and the trader has the option to buy or sell the asset within a particular period, the transaction is called an *option*.

Borrowers consist of individuals (often referred to as households), small and large businesses, major corporations, and all levels of government. Interestingly, the list of lenders consists of the same group. We do not differentiate between domestic and global participants here because it does not matter. The household that is lending loanable funds to a financial intermediary in the United States can live anywhere in the world. The majority of borrowers and lenders in a given country, however, operate within that country. The same reasons that necessitate the existence of intermediaries in a country also necessitate the existence of international intermediaries. In addition, international transactions have to overcome differences in nationality, culture, language, and distance.

At any given time many people are both lenders and borrowers. People have both bonds and mortgage. They may have a college fund, while also financing their car. In general, younger people are net borrowers and older people are net lenders. Financial intermediaries help to facilitate these transactions through *financial instruments,* which are explained in the following sections.

Financial Instruments

U.S. Treasury bills (T-bills) are the most liquid financial instrument. They are issued by the U.S. government and are short-term debt obligations of one year or less. Historically, the largest holders of T-bills, in descending order, are commercial banks, other financial intermediaries, businesses, foreign investors, state and local governments, and U.S. households.

Money market instruments are securities and investments by private enterprises. Other money market instruments include Treasury bills, U.S. Government agency discount notes, municipal tax anticipation notes, and commercial papers. They are the most liquid private instruments. Their short-term maturity makes their interest rates more stable. Like other private instruments, these also have risk.

Commercial papers are issued by well-known firms and financial institutions. They have higher interest rates than T-bills and have lower risk than other private instruments. Commercial papers allow major firms to raise their needed funds directly; they act as their own intermediaries.

Bankers' acceptances are financial instruments created by banks to facilitate transactions between international borrowers and lenders. They are like checks written in one country to be cashed in another. They are widely used by importers and exporters.

Repurchase agreements were mostly used by large corporations for cash management for very short terms, up to two weeks; however, at present, state and local governments as well as modest-sized businesses use them. The firm can buy a financial instrument, for example, a T-bill, and the bank agrees to buy back the instrument at a higher price, which is equal to the interest earned on the value of the instrument during that period. The instrument is used as collateral.

Negotiable bank certificates of deposit is a fixed maturity instrument with a higher interest rate than a savings account. The longer the maturity term or the larger the deposit, the higher will be the interest rate.

Eurodollars are U.S. dollars that are in banks outside of the U.S. With the growth of emerging market economies, these dollars are not necessarily in European banks anymore.

Capital Market Instruments

U.S. Treasury Securities are intermediate to long-term bonds issued by the federal government. The primary purpose of this instrument has been to finance U.S. budget deficits since the late twentieth century.

Federal Funds are overnight loans that banks deposit with the Federal Reserve banks. The Fed requires banks to deposit a certain percentage of their funds at the Fed to safeguard them against a run on the bank, as well as a method of controlling the supply of money. When a commercial bank reserve is less than the required amount, it borrows the shortfall from another bank with excess reserve at the Fed. The interest rate charged on these overnight loans is called the *federal funds rate*. The federal funds rate is a gauge of the tightness of the money supply in the economy.

U.S. Government Agency Securities are intermediate to long-term bonds, but issued by government-sponsored agencies or the federal government. Some of the agency securities are not explicitly guaranteed by the U.S. government, such as those issued by small business administration and housing and urban development.

State and local government bonds (municipal bonds) are intermediate- to long-term bonds, which are issued by municipalities and state governments. The earnings of these bonds are exempt from federal income tax and usually from state income tax within the issuing state. The rating and interest rates of these bonds depend on the health of the economy of the city or state that issues them.

Stocks are corporation equities. Although trade in stocks is the largest component of capital market assets, new stock issues are not a major source of acquiring capital by businesses in the United States. Stocks fluctuate more than corporate bonds, but are also more liquid.

Corporate bonds are intermediate- to long-term instruments issued by large and reputable corporations. The most common corporate bonds pay interest biannually.

Convertible bonds are corporate funds that can be converted to equity at a given rate of conversion.

Mortgages are long-term loans for the purchase of land and/or buildings, which are used as collateral. Residential mortgages are issued by commercial banks and savings institutions, whereas business mortgages are offered by life insurance companies, as well as commercial banks. Residential mortgages have been supported by the U.S. government, which provides liquid secondary national mortgage markets through the Federal National Mortgage Association (FNMA, pronounced as Fannie Mae), Federal Home Loan Mortgage Corporation (FHLMC, pronounced Freddie Mac), and Government National Mortgage Association (GNMA, pronounced Ginny Mae).

Information Asymmetry

Access to information is important in economics. An important prerequisite for the operation of markets under perfect competition is complete access to information. There is an asymmetry in access to information between financial intermediaries and the general public, which necessitates regulations and disclosure requirements. There are three issues that still tilt the scale in favor of the financial institutions. First, disclosure requirements are not strong enough to force intermediaries to reveal all their information. Second, in an attempt to maximize their profits the intermediaries introduce new innovations, all of which are designed to benefit the institutions. Third, the playing field is not level. Financial intermediaries have professional and educated employees, while the majority of the public are amateurs at best. Furthermore, while employees of these institutions are experts in their field and are engaged in dealing in the same or similar matters, the investors, by contrast, seldom engage in financial transactions. For example, a typical person may buy one or two homes in his life. Even people who are investing regularly have limited experience in all of the different types of financial arrangements available. Consequently, deregulation of financial institutions causes serious crises, such as the savings and loans crisis of the late 1980s or the housing crisis of 2008.

Information asymmetry in the financial market is compared to that of the *lemon cars* in the used car market by George Akerlof, Nobel Prize laureate.[1] A typical buyer of used cars may buy a handful of cars in his life while a used car dealer sells substantially more than that each year. The dealer has better access to mechanics that can determine the problems of lemon cars. Myers and Majluf, and Greenwald, Stiglitz, and Weiss provide the application of Akerlof's theory in financial markets.[2,3] Financial institutions, by contrast, face the problem of adverse selection. *Adverse selection* is a type of information asymmetry. The borrower knows his or her personal financial situation. A borrower with bad credit would be willing to accept less favorable conditions, while not disclosing his or her poor credit history. A borrower who has no intention of paying back the loan would not divulge his intention. Adverse selection, therefore, occurs before the transaction. The party that has high risk or plans on not repaying the loan is more eager to obtain a loan, even if the terms are harsher than normal, such as in the majority of payday loans.

Moral Hazard

Moral hazard occurs when the action of one party has a detrimental effect on the other party in a transaction. Moral hazard arises after the transaction, when the borrower engages in riskier endeavors than the one for which the loan was requested. Moral hazard and adverse selection are not necessarily caused by individuals. Financial institutions and corporations could also be the culprit. Examples abound, but it is sufficient here to mention Enron, which in 2000 was the seventh largest corporation in the United States.

Interestingly, financial intermediaries have emerged in part to eliminate, or at least to reduce, the adverse effects of transactions with unknown individuals and to increase information availability. Obtaining information about products, buyers, sellers, borrowers, and lenders is expensive. Financial intermediaries reduce the cost of information by acquiring expertise and lower the risk by providing permanency to the transaction; they would not fold after few transactions. Although financial intermediaries provide a valuable service, increase the availability of information, reduce transaction costs, and make the financial markets more competitive and efficient, because of their profit motive and asymmetric access to information and expertise, it is necessary, if not vital, for governments to regulate their industry and to track their activities.

Power of Financial Intermediaries

Intermediaries, both financial and nonfinancial, have several advantages over individuals when it comes to making transactions. Some of the advantages of financial intermediaries, such as banks, are addressed briefly. A bank collects and processes information about individuals and firms. They are given the authority to request financial and private information from their clients, both depositors and borrowers. Because of the large volume of transactions, banks can afford to hire experts in statistics and modeling to forecast the probability of default and to separate low-risk clients from high-risk ones. They can deny loans to high-risk clients or require higher interest rates and shorter terms. Some intermediaries, such as mortgage lenders, can also require insurance on riskier loans. All lenders can and do require collateral, which reduces risk, and provides assurances that the loan is used appropriately and that prudent steps are taken to protect the original sum, such as requiring insurance on an automobile, home, or factory. *Collateral* is a good of known value that is promised to the lender in case the borrower defaults. The lender can legally take possession of the collateral in the event of default.

Regulation is Different than Smothering Competition

Discussion of the power of financial intermediaries and the need for regulation might lead the reader to believe that competition is not good. Somehow, the presence of regulation has been associated with curbing competition. The types of regulations addressed here are those that require sharing information, disclosure of terms and conditions, honesty in presentation of financial documents, transparency, and the like. We do not advocate the type of regulation that limits or hinders competition. Indeed, financial regulations have allowed national and international banks to operate in small towns and outside of their states, reducing the monopoly power of small-town banks that existed until the end of the twentieth century.

Definition

Monopoly is a market structure in which a single producer provides the good or the service. For example, a single bank in a small town is a monopoly.

The advocates of free markets that equate regulations with hindrance of competition would argue that issues, such as the adverse selection problem, can be solved by the market mechanism. The problem with adverse selection is the discrepancy of information between buyers and sellers, and also between those who professionally participate in the market and those who only participate occasionally. Market mechanisms would resolve the latter problem because the economic profit made by a dealer or institution would signal to others to enter the market, which would force prices down and eliminate economic profit, leaving only the accounting profit or a reasonable return for labor and capital. While this would occur in larger markets, it would not be possible in small communities, or when there is a giant player, or several large institutions. In small communities, in particular, the demand would not be large enough to warrant a sufficient number of institutions to establish the requirements for perfect competition in a free market. At best, markets will be somewhere between a state of monopolistic competition and monopoly. Another issue is the lack of free mobility. Free mobility refers to the ability to enter and exit from market without obstacles.

Definition

Monopolistic competition is a market structure in which few producers of goods or services dominate the market but there are many smaller producers as well. In the monopolistic competition the goods or services are differentiable, which could be real or perceived.

Even when there is a sufficient number of traders on both sides, some, if not most, of the other requirements of a perfectly competitive market, such as the availability of information or mobility of resources, may not exist. Our focus here is the availability of information. Private companies, such as Standard and Poor or Moody, provide information about various types of savers and lenders and publish a variety of financial information, such as investment histories and balance sheets. Firms and individuals would subscribe to their publications to increase their access information and to reduce their uncertainty. Once the data are published, it is not that difficult for nonsubscribers to access the data. These free-riders circumvent the solution. Had these non-subscribers paid for the data, the price of data would have been higher due to increased demand. In the presence of free-riders, the data, like any other underpriced good, is underproduced, thus the practice harms the entire market.

CHAPTER 11

Equilibrium in the Goods Market: IS Model

Introduction

It might seem strange to have a chapter on equilibrium in the goods market in a text on money. Money, however, would not have been necessary if there were not a goods market, and speaking of equilibrium in the money market without discussing what it would take for equilibrium in the goods market would be meaningless. The foundations of the quantity theory were implicitly based on equilibrium in both the goods and money markets. Equilibrium in the goods market means that the money market must also be in equilibrium. Departures from equilibrium in either market would disturb the entire economy and would cause changes in both the goods and money markets. In stable economies, such disturbances would fade away, like ripples on the water after a rock is dropped in a pond.

At the macro level all goods and services are aggregated. The aggregate market for goods and services must be at equilibrium. Therefore, it is necessary to identify the factors that affect the equilibrium. Consequently, it is a major component of macroeconomic theory. The aggregate market for goods and services is at equilibrium if the supply and demand for all the goods and services, in all sectors of the economy, are at equilibrium. In other words, the supply of every good is equal to the demand for the good at its equilibrium price. One of the main contributors to macroeconomic analysis of the twentieth century was John Maynard Keynes. Many important economists devoted years to elaborating on Keynes' theories,[1] as depicted in the *General Theory of Employment and Interest*, and trying to validate or disprove them. One notable such researcher was Hicks.[2] In his econometrics-based article, Hicks used IS to label the goods market equilibrium curve and LL to label the money market equilibrium curve. Later, LL was modified to LM, which has been used ever since. We will discuss the IS model in this chapter, while addressing the LM model in the next chapter. The IS–LM model is the foundation of modern macroeconomic analysis and, thus, the principal tool for obtaining information for formulation of the fiscal and monetary policies. IS schedule is discussed in this chapter, while the LM schedule is the subject of Chapter 12.

Definition

IS curve is the loci of interest rate–output sets for which the goods market is in equilibrium.

Goods Market

For the sake of brevity and space, the word *goods* is used to refer to *goods and services*, that is, to represent all the goods and services produced and traded in the economy. To make the analysis less complicated, it is customary to assume, at least momentarily, that the prices of goods are constant. It is also common to state that the prices are given. This assumption implies that there exists an idle production capacity in output indicating that the output can increase without pressure or the need to increase prices. This assumption is actually a reality during recession, which was the main focus of Keynes' work. In economic terms, the supply of goods is *perfectly elastic* under this assumption.

Definition

The supply of a good is *perfectly elastic* if it can increase without limit in response to an increase in demand.

When supply is perfectly elastic, demand is the driving force in the economy and determines the price, and hence the quantity produced in the goods market. At equilibrium, supply and demand are equal, unintended inventories are zero, and actual consumption equals planned consumption. Aggregate demand for goods consists of consumption and investment (C + I). Therefore aggregate demand is

$$AD = C + I \qquad (11.1)$$

Note that for simplicity in this model there is not any government or foreign trade. Since prices do not change under the assumption of excess production capacity, producers correct their production level by following the changes in their inventory. Unintended excess inventory signals the need to reduce output. Adding government, G, and net exports, NX, to the model results in the open-economy version with sizeable government.

$$AD = C + I + G + NX \qquad (11.2)$$

At equilibrium, aggregate demand equals aggregate output, Y.

$$Y = AD = C + I + G + NX \qquad (11.3)$$

When the economy is not at equilibrium, there is an unintended inventory, UI, which can be positive or negative, depending on the nature of disequilibrium or the stage of the business cycle.

$$UI = Y - AD \qquad (11.4)$$

When UI > 0, firms will cut back on investment, production, overtime, and possibly, the actual labor force.

According to Keynes,[1] consumption is a function of income, which is also shown by Y, because the value of the output in an economy is equal to its income.

$$C = C_0 + MPC(Y) \qquad 0 < (MPC) < 1 \text{ and } C_0 > 0 \qquad (11.5)$$

MPC represents the *marginal propensity to consume.*

Definition

Marginal Propensity to Consume is the change in consumption due to one unit change in income.

MPC is assumed to be positive, indicating that at least part of the income is used for consumption, and less than one, which implies that consumption out of additional income does not exceed the extra income. At zero income, it is still necessary to consume some positive amount to survive. This subsistence level is shown by C_0. The portion of a dollar that is not consumed is saved, which is assumed to be invested. Although MPC is customarily for consumers, one can think of MPC for a government as well. It can be argued that when a government has a budget deficit, its MPC > 1.

Therefore, the *marginal propensity to save* is

$$\text{MPS} = 1 - \text{MPC} \qquad 0 < \text{MPS} < 1 \qquad (11.6)$$

Total savings is the difference between earnings and consumption.

$$S = Y - C \qquad (11.7)$$

Figure 11.1 provides a simple visual presentation of equilibrium between income and consumption. The x axis represents income, Y, and the y axis represents consumption, C, as well as aggregate demand, AD. The consumption line intersects the y axis at C_0, or the subsistence level, and slopes upward according to the magnitude of MPC. The forty-five-degree line, where AD = Y, represents all the points for which income, Y, is equal to consumption, C, or aggregate demand, AD, depending on which one is the focus of the attention. Therefore, the point where the consumption line intersects the forty-five-degree line, E_c, represents equilibrium in a closed economy with no government sector, while the point at which aggregate demand intersects the forty-five-degree line, E_{AD}, represents

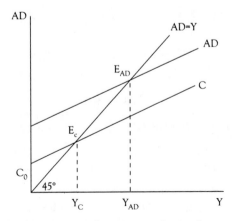

Figure 11.1. Consumption and aggregate demand.

the equilibrium when the government sector is present. If the aggregate demand includes trade then the model represents an open economy. The income–consumption pair in the closed economy is designated by Y_c and C_0 on their respective axes, while the income–aggregate demand pairs are shown by Y_{AD} and AD_0, respectively. In the case of a general model with investment, government, and trade, investment is equal to savings.

The combined graph for the closed and open economy serves other purposes as well. Because income and output are the same and are depicted on the x axis, the vertical distance between the consumption line and the forty-five-degree line for any given point, is the difference between consumption and income, or savings. The underlying assumption is that the economy is operating under the perfectly competitive environment. From the graph, it is apparent that only at the equilibrium point E_{AD}, savings is equal to investment plus government plus net trade. Assuming, for the sake of simplicity and clarity, that government expenditure and trade are zero, or at least cancel each other out, the line at the top becomes equal to C + I. In the range to the left of equilibrium E_{AD} the combined values of C + I are greater than income; therefore, the unintended inventory must be negative. In the range to the right of equilibrium point E_{AD}, the combined values of C + I are less than income, so the unintended inventory, UI, is positive. Therefore, to the left of E_{AD}, investment must increase, whereas to the right of it, investment must decrease, thereby correcting for underproduction and overproduction, respectively, and returning the economy to the equilibrium point.

An increase in income would increase consumption by the amount of MPC times the magnitude of change in income. The contribution of Keynes is that the consumption of one person is someone else's income; therefore, an increase in consumption would result in an increase in income, which in turn would trigger another round of increase in consumption proportionate to the MPC. The iterations continue, but each time the magnitude decreases because MPC is smaller than one. This is the *multiplier effect*. The sum of all increases in income can be shown to equal the inverse of the marginal propensity to save.

$$\Delta Y = \frac{1}{1 - MPC} = \frac{1}{MPS} \qquad (11.8)$$

Definition

Multiplier effect refers to the successive rounds of income–consumption generated by an initial increase in consumption, investment, or government expenditures.

As marginal propensity to consume increases, the denominator decreases, which produces a greater multiplier effect. The opposite is true about marginal propensity to save. This paradoxical outcome is known as the *paradox of thrift*.

Definition

Paradox of thrift refers to the notion that an increase in individual savings contracts the economy due to a reduction in the multiplier effect.

The multiplier effect highlights the fact that a dollar spent in an economy continues to augment income and consumption, although, at incrementally smaller magnitudes until it becomes negligible. The origin of the initial increase can be from a multitude of sources, such as government stimulus spending or a bank lending part of the money deposited with the bank in a savings account. This augmenting effect of a given expenditure is the essence of fiscal policy.[3] A common fallacy is that fiscal stimulus must be for a *useful* product. It is totally irrelevant how the new income becomes available to the economy. However, a useful product has value in its own right. What makes the multiplier effective is the pursuit of consumption–income iterations as pointed out by Keynes:[1]

> If the treasury were to fill old bottles with banknotes, bury them at suitable depths in disused coal mines, which are then filled up to the surface with town rubbish, and leave it to private enterprise on well-tried principles of Laissez-faire to dig the notes up again (the right to do so being obtained, of course, by tendering for leases of the note-bearing territory), there need be no more unemployment and, with the help of repercussions, the real income of the community, and its capital wealth, would probably become a good deal greater than it actually is.

The Federal government can operate under budget deficit. Therefore, it is possible for the government to stimulate the economy by running a budget deficit. When the economy is at full employment it cannot produce more than it is already producing. The main application of fiscal stimulus is during recessionary periods, when there exists unemployment of workers and capital, in the form of excess capacity in all sectors of the economy. There are data on industry and capacity utilization (Federal Reserve Board) and quarterly survey data on plant capacity utilization that provide estimates of underutilization in the manufacturing sector (U.S. Census Bureau).

When part of the generated income is taxed, the effect of the multiplier is reduced. When income is taxed the income–consumption iterations are smaller compared to the case when there were no taxes. In this case, the available disposable income is smaller than the earned income, and thus, the multiplier effect is smaller. This notion would be true only if the amount that is taxed is taken out of the circulation, which is not the case in reality. The only difference that the introduction of government in the model accomplishes is that part of the generated income becomes government revenue; therefore, part of the consumption that is made possible by the new income is through the public sector. One might argue that the presence of government actually increases the multiplier effect, instead of reducing it. The MPC for consumers is between zero and one and some estimate it to be about 90%[4] or higher.[5] At the same time, the MPC for government is seldom less than one. In recent years it has actually exceeded one, with deficit financing. Consequently, the multiplier is higher in the presence of government than when it is excluded.

The Goods Market and the IS Curve

In the more general model we have

$$Y = C + I + G + NX \qquad (11.9)$$

Originally, we assumed everything was exogenously determined and used this model to explain equilibrium in the economy. Then, we took a more realistic approach and made consumption a function of income and derived the multiplier effect that explains the consequences of the income–consumption–income sequence. We continued assuming investment, government expenditures, and net exports to be exogenously determined. In reality, that is not the case. Even government expenditure depends on economic productivity to some extent, although it seems that the legislators can simply vote to spend or not spend money. This cannot be further from reality as the budget wrangling of the years 2011–2013 has demonstrated. Similarly, net exports, or more precisely the import component of it, is definitely a function of a country's income. As the income of a country increases, the demand for all goods increases, including the demand for imports. Customarily, exports are considered more of a function of the importing country's income, rather than depending on the economic forces of the exporting country. Although this might be acceptable for large countries or countries with small export sectors, it is not necessarily true of countries like Singapore with a substantial export sector. For the time being, however, we will focus on investment and link it to the state of the economy.

Demand for Investment

The discussion of the internal rate of return in Chapter 7 demonstrated that as the interest rate increases, the number of investments that remain profitable declines. This suggests a downward-sloping investment function. To make investment decisions endogenous within economy, the inverse relationship between the interest rate and investment can be presented in a linear format as follows:

$$I = I_0 - b_i \qquad b > 0 \qquad\qquad (11.10)$$

where I is the planned investment, I_0 is the maximum amount of investment per period, which can happen only if the interest rate is zero, i is the interest rate, and b is the responsiveness of investment to interest rate. During recessionary periods, b would be small due to the existence of excess capacity. During booms, the responsiveness would become larger until the production capacity of the economy is reached. After that point, reductions in interest rate cannot increase investment due to bottlenecks in some or all sectors of the economy. If the variables were measured in logarithmic values, b would have been the elasticity of investment with respect

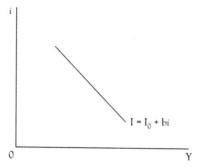

Figure 11.2. Investment function.

to the interest rate. Note that I_0 is completely independent of the interest rate. Figure 11.2 depicts this investment function.

The IS Model

Generally with government and trade, the model is written as follows:

$$AD = C + I + G + NX \qquad (11.11)$$

Substituting for C and I we obtain

$$AD = C_0 + MPC\ Y + I_0 - b_i + G + NX \qquad (11.12)$$

By assumption, the following components of the model are exogenous to the system, and therefore, group them together and treat them as constant

$$A = C_0 + I_0 + G + NX \qquad (11.13)$$

Textbooks dedicated to macroeconomics treat government expenditures and trade endogenously by expressing them as functions of income and other economic factors. Customarily, government expenditure and trade models are specified in two parts: one part is exogenous, while the other part is endogenous, similar to the consumption and investment modes.

$$AD = A + MPC\ Y - b_i \qquad (11.14)$$

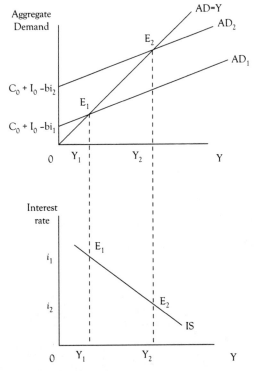

Figure 11.3. IS schedule.

An astute student would notice that we did not include taxes or the marginal tax rate in the model. This is permissible if the marginal propensity to consume for individuals and government is the same. When the government MPC is greater than or less than one, the above model yields a different estimate.

An increase in income will increase aggregate demand by a smaller magnitude, because MPC < 1 and an increase in the interest rate will decrease aggregate demand. The relationship between the interest rate and income, which is equal to aggregate demand by definition, is depicted as the IS curve, as shown in Figure 11.3.

It is important to realize that there are two variables in Equation 11.12, namely, income and interest rate. Hicks derived the IS schedule,[2] which relates income/output to the interest rate, by realizing that allowing the interest rate to change from state I to state II would only cause a shift in the AD, which is still a function of income, as in Figure 11.3. Transferring this to part b of the graph provides two points, each of which reflects an interest rate–income combination, which represents an equilibrium point in the goods market. Connecting the two points creates an IS schedule. The IS curve represents the combinations of interest rate and output where the goods market is in equilibrium. Because an increase in the interest rate reduces income/output, the IS curve is downward sloping.

CHAPTER 12

Equilibrium in the Financial System: LM Model

Introduction

Equilibrium in the goods market is necessary, but not sufficient for equilibrium in the overall economy. To achieve overall equilibrium in the economy, it is also necessary to have equilibrium in the money market.

Recall that Keynes demonstrated the link between interest rate and demand for money. We have also shown that during inflationary periods, the price level, that is, the prices of all the goods including money, increase. Because interest rate is the price of money, it is necessary to use the real interest rate in economic analysis instead of the nominal interest rate. Here, the word *real* is used in contrast to the word *nominal*. The nominal interest rate is equal to the real interest rate plus the inflation rate. Because it is the purchasing power of money that is important for people, a theory of demand for money is actually a theory of demand for real, rather than nominal balances. To derive the LM schedule, we need to make the same assumption as the classical quantity theorists and equate money supply with money demand.

Definition

The *LM schedule* is the loci of combinations of interest rates and incomes that result in equilibrium in the money market.

Demand for Money Revisited

As demonstrated in Chapter 4, the demand for real money is a function of real income and the real interest rate. In order to obtain *real* values, *nominal* values are divided by the price level or price index. Sometimes, for the sake of clarity, it is customary to use the term *real money balances* instead of *real money*. A person with more income is expected to demand more real money balances to meet his financial obligations. Everyone holds less money as the opportunity cost of holding it increases. The opportunity cost of holding money is the foregone interest. Therefore, as the real interest rate increases, the demand for money decreases. Thus, we formulate the demand for money as a function of income and the interest rate as follows:

$$M^d = mY - ni \quad m, n > 0 \qquad (12.1)$$

where M^d is the demand for real money, m represents the responsiveness of demand for money to income, and n shows the sensitivity of money demand to the interest rate. The negative coefficient on the interest rate indicates that the demand for real money is a downward-sloping function like demand for other normal goods. We will use this property when depicting the LM schedule. On the other hand, the coefficient for income is positive, indicating a direct relationship between income and demand for money.

Supply of Money Revisited

The demand for money by itself cannot determine the interest rate. It provides a set of points that indicate the amount of money demanded for alternative interest rates, but it is unable to determine the specific interest rate at equilibrium. To determine the interest rate at equilibrium, one must also know the supply of money. Since the Federal Reserve controls the supply of money, the curve is assumed to be vertical. A vertical supply line indicates a perfectly inelastic supply curve. In other words, the Fed is not influenced by the economy in deciding the supply of money, which is definitely not the case in the long run. However, an inelastic money supply schedule is not unrealistic, at least in the short run. In monetary policy,[1] it is important to sustain a steady and predictable strategy. Therefore, some argue that it is better not to react to every little movement and change in the market. In the short run, changes in the supply of money would affect the economy, especially if the changes are unexpected. An increase in the supply of money would increase economic activity, output, and income, although these are not affected by the supply of money in the long run. However, timing a policy-induced change in the money supply in order to achieve a particular objective is difficult and mistakes can make the matter worse. The recommendation of the majority of economists is that the supply of money should be isolated from random market fluctuations.

Other Ways for Supplying Money

Customarily, when we think of money, we think about the bills and coins printed and minted at the Treasury and under the directive of the Federal Reserve. However, there is another way to create or supply money, which takes place through the banking system. The process is not that much different than the way the multiplier effect functions.

When some money is deposited at a bank, chances are that the deposit will be kept for a while. Even when monthly income is deposited in a checking account, half of it, on the average, stays in the bank for month. The deposit can be your paycheck deposited into your checking account, which you gradually spend over the course of the month. Assuming a steady stream of expenditure, you will deplete 1/30th of your income each day, assuming you spend all of it and do not save any of it for later. If you saved some for the future, the money creation of the bank actually becomes stronger. Under the assumption of a constant flow of expenditures, the bank knows that you will spend 1/30th of your income on the first day and keep 29/30 of your income. On the second day, you will spend another 1/30th and keep the remaining 28/30th until the last day, when you spend the remaining 1/30th of your income. The bank can lend your unspent money for up to the number of days you keep it in your account before spending it. The main revenue of the banks is from the differential in interest rate they pay when they borrow and the rate they charge when they lend. The resulting revenue pays for the salaries of employees, utilities, advertisement, building, etc. as well as for the capital the bank invested. The money that the bank lends out is like a new supply of money that is injected in the economy. The extra money created is no different than freshly minted money by the Treasury Department.

Since banks receive interest on the money they lend they would like to lend as much of the money at their possession as possible. Miscalculation by banks or an increase in the rate or the amounts of withdrawals will result in shortage of cash at the bank. When a bank becomes insolvent it causes panic in the public, which causes an increase in the rate and the magnitude of withdrawals. Some people would attempt to close their accounts and remove all their money, in spite of the fact that deposits are insured by the Federal Deposit Insurance Corporation for up to $250,000. A problem in one bank might erode the faith of the public in the banking system and there might be a run on the banks. Periodical runs on the bank as a result of failure to keep sufficient cash in the bank to be able to honor higher than expected withdrawals was one main reason for the creation of the Federal Reserve Bank, as explained in Chapter 5. The Federal Reserve Bank has the authority to force banks to maintain a percentage of their deposits at the bank and/or at the Federal Reserve Bank of the region, known as the *reserve*. When the supply of money exceeds the desired level, the Fed increases the *required reserve*. The Fed decreases the required reserve when there is a shortage of money. By changing the magnitude of the required reserve the Fed is able to control the supply of money, which allows us to assume a vertical short run money supply in spite of the ability of banks to create money independently from the Treasury Department. The Fed also uses the required reserve or the *overnight rate* that is charged when banks borrow from each other and the Fed, to meet the reserve requirement to implement monetary policy. When a bank lends money it increases the amount of money since the owner of the original deposit can use his or her money for transaction just as the recipient of the loan would.

Derivation of the LM Schedule

We have shown that the goods market aggregate demand is a function of interest rate and consumption, and that change in one or the other would cause a change in the output/income level. In order to isolate the effect of the interest rate, we changed the value of consumption and traced the changes in another diagram to link income and the interest rate, deriving the IS schedule.

The demand for money is also a function of two variables, the interest rate and income. In order to isolate the effect of the interest rate, we allow the income level to change as in the left panel of Figure 12.1 and trace the effect of the change in another figure to obtain the LM schedule, as in the right panel of Figure 12.1. The two lines in the left panel correspond to two different levels of income, Y_1 and Y_2. Since the left panel does not represent income on either axis change in Y from lower value, Y_1, to higher value, Y_2 causes an upward shift in the line. The shift in income increases the demand for money, which raises the interest rate from i_1 to i_2, see left panel Figure 12.1. The intersection of the inelastic money supply curve, the vertical line, with the two demand curves yields two points. These two points, which are associated with the two values of income, Y1 and Y2, provide two points on the LM curve in the right panel of Figure 12.1. Connecting the two points provides the LM schedule.

Consequently, depicting the interest rate and income in one graph would indicate that the result of an increase in the interest rate is an increase in income. Therefore, the LM schedule is an upward sloping curve.

To become familiar with the effects of shifts in IS and LM curves, it is recommended that the reader practice by following the examples provided above. For both IS and LM, steeper curves indicate larger and more force-ful reaction to a change in interest rate.

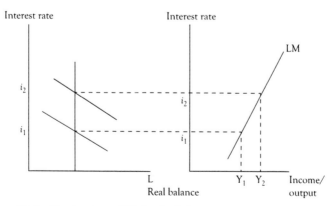

Figure 12.1. Derivation of LM schedule.

Equilibrium in the Goods and Money Market

The IS schedule depicts the points along which pairs of the interest rate and income result in equilibrium in the goods market. The LM schedule depicts the points along which pairs of the interest rate and income are at equilibrium in the money market. Combining these, as in Figure 12.2, provides the unique pair of income and the corresponding interest rate, where both the market for goods and the market for money are at equilibrium, which corresponds to the intersection of the two curves, similar to the intersection of supply and demand in a single market case.

In order to determine the derivations of the IS and LM schedules, we made the simplifying assumption of constant prices and the ability of producers to increase their output without the need for a price increase. These assumptions are usually the characteristics of an underemployed and underutilized economy, which prevails during a recessionary period. Technically, except for when the economy is at full employment, there is always excess capacity. There is excess capacity when an economy slows down, when it is in recession, and during the recovery.

The Dynamics of Market Equilibrium

Changes in the factors that affect the IS or LM schedules will result in shifts in the IS or LM curves. An increase in investment would shift IS up and to the right from IS_1 to IS_2 in Figure 11.2 as well as in Figure 12.2. In the case of Figure 11.2, it is not clear what happens to either the interest rate or income as a result of the increase in investment. However, in Figure 12.2,

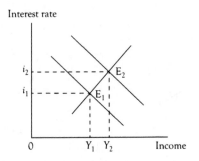

Figure 12.2. IS–LM schedule and market equilibrium.

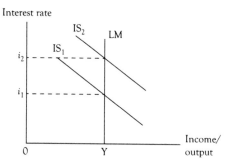

Figure 12.3. A vertical LM schedule.

it is clear that the result is an increase in income from Y_1 to Y_2 and an increase in interest rate from i_1 to i_2. The market equilibrium moves from E_1 to E_2.

Referring to Figure 11.2, the magnitude of the change in investment is measured on the horizontal axis, which is the same as the horizontal distance between IS_1 to IS_2 in Figure 12.2. This is larger than the increase in income, which is the gap between Y_1 and Y_2. The reason is that the investment responsiveness, represented by b, is less than one. Another reason for the difference in magnitude is due to the slope of the LM schedule. If the slope of the LM was zero, that is, the LM curve was flat and horizontal, then the entire shift in IS as a result of an increase in investment would have been transferred to income and the increase in income would have been equal to that of the investment. In the opposite extreme in an economy with a vertical LM schedule, an autonomous increase in investment will not increase the output or income although it will still shift the IS curve to the right and up, as in Figure 12.3.

A vertical IS curve means that the link between the interest rate and income/output is broken and that changes in the interest rate would not affect income. Ironically, a shift in the IS curve in this situation will change income by an equal amount, but in this case, the shift in IS must be induced by something other than the interest rate.

CHAPTER 13

Conclusion

The discussion of money plays a major role in economics. I have tried to not make this book a boring list of definitions and rules about money. To this end, I start with the quantity theory of money. The quantity theory is about the demand for money. It provides a plausible explanation for behavior of money and the response of economy to changes in money. Like most early attempts to unravel a complex phenomenon, the quantity theory had some shortcomings. Later developments remedy some of the problems and set the stage for a major contribution by Keynes, who combined many of the existing knowledge on the subject and augmented it with contributions of his own. Keynes' work encouraged active government participation in the economy. By the time Keynes finished his first book, the concept of a planned economy was already well established in socialist countries and government involvement in economic affairs was not a new idea. However, Keynes' recommendation for governmental intervention in the economy was confined to the market economy and the capitalist system. Possibly one of the greatest misunderstandings of the Keynesian theory is the notion that it leads to communism. The second half of the twentieth century witnessed a substantial increase in government involvement in the economies on both sides of the Atlantic Ocean and elsewhere. The share of government from GDP in the United States has been above 30% for most of the past half century. The share of government from GDP is even higher in many other countries. However, Keynes recommended a greater role for the government in the economy to combat recession and to make the ebb and flow of business cycles less prominent, which is far less than the actual extent of government engagement in the economy in many parts of the world today.

Keynes pointed out that during economic downturns there is an excess capacity in the economy, which can be eliminated through government intervention. An initial government expansionary expenditure will set the multiplier effect into action and lead to successive rounds of consumption–income cycles and increased demand, thus, eliminating the excess capacity and providing economic prosperity. The Keynesian theory is the focus of fiscal policy, but to understand the Keynesian theory and the multiplier effect, it is necessary to study his explanation of demand for money and the different motives that initiate the demand.

Inherent in economic activities and monetary transactions is the notion of risk and uncertainty. Because the ability to incorporate risk and uncertainty were not developed until much later, the earlier economic theories could not integrate them. The first attempts for incorporating risk were through its effect on the interest rate. By the 1960s, the interest rate was a main factor in both fiscal and monetary theories.

The struggle to identify the role of money in economic growth resulted in classification of money according to its liquidity. A lower number, such as M1, designates greater liquidity. Deciding what is money and what role it plays in the economy is important. The policy implications of the validity of the explanations provided by fiscal and monetary policy are enormous. How money functions and affects the economy determine whether the fiscal or monetary policy is correct, which in turn determines what course of action, if any, the government should take. During the twentieth century the debate on the subject was hottest during the Keynes era and the Friedman era. The importance of the role of money in the economy and the ensuing support for fiscal or monetary policy has boiled down into the following question: "Does money matter?" The reader would realize that this question is not addressed in any detail in this book about money. The reason is that the answer to the question is the foundation of the debate about the role and importance of fiscal and monetary policies. This book is designed to familiarize the reader with the fundamentals of money in order for the reader to be able to better understand fiscal and monetary policies.

An integral part of the discussion about the power and the ability of fiscal and monetary policies is the question of who creates and controls the supply of money. The basic mechanics of the process was addressed in this book, but briefly. Undoubtedly, the Federal Reserve Bank plays a major role in creation and control of the supply of money but the banks, directly, and the public, indirectly, play important roles as well. A more important question than who creates the money is who controls it. Having control over money implies that the supply of money can be used as a policy instrument to achieve economic objectives. Here too, the advocates of fiscal policy clash with the supporters of monetary policy. Both groups agree that money is powerful, but maybe more in the sense of a Pandora's Box. Money must be important or it would not be used to influence the economy. Therefore, the debate is over the issue of whether it is possible to control the power of this monster once it is summoned. One of the differences between the advocates of the fiscal and monetary policy is the degree of control and predictability of the influence of money in the economy.

Governments have been responsible for controlling money supply for centuries. One method of controlling money is to control the physical currency. This is not as easy as it might seem, due to the fact that the economic conditions and the institutional norms of the country determine how rapidly the currency in circulation exchanges hands. In other words, the actual amount of money depends on its velocity, which is not controlled by the government. In addition, in a capitalist country, the government has to deal with private banks and allow them to operate with as little mandates and regulations as possible. Therefore, the government's control over the money created by banks is, for the most part, indirect and through the manipulation of the interest rate, which in turn is controlled by selling and buying of bonds.

Ever since governments became engaged in minting coins, the precious metal value of the coins was less than their face values. When paper money became common, governments were not required to maintain proportionate amounts of precious metals in reserves anymore. Finally, when the true fiat money was created, it became evident that there never was any need for any precious metal backing for money in order for the money to perform its job, a fact that was known to the cowry shell users three millenniums before. Even when the dominant form of money contained precious metals, money was created without the backing of precious metals anytime someone placed his money with someone else for safe keeping and that person loaned part of the money. The move from (partially) gold-backed currency to completely fiat money is important because it increased the government's power and control over the monetary system of the country. Consequently, governments have complete power and authority over creation of money, and thus, the full power to exert monetary policy.

The abolishment of precious metal backing of currency was more important for international transactions than for the domestic ones. Therefore, the greatest problem and resistance to conversion was at the international level. The global dominance of the United States after World War II had two opposing effects on this matter. On one hand, it seemed that without the backing of gold, United States could do anything it wanted but on the other hand, its dominance was seen as a source of stability and security in financial markets and the dominance of the United States' currency was welcomed by many of the industrialized countries.

The Keynesian theory of fiscal policy had gained validity and respect after the Great Depression. However, its dominance had to wait until World War II ended. For a while, the accepted norm was government intervention in the economy through both fiscal and monetary policy. A widely accepted practice was to manipulate the economy using fiscal policy, including the practice of deficit financing, and monetary policy, including the creation of money either directly by printing new money or more subtly, through the money creation abilities of the banking system.

After it became evident that the trade-off between unemployment and inflation does not work and the higher inflation rates of the 1970s seemed to be the norm, the new monetary theory recommendations of less government intervention in the economy gained more respect. The historical evidence of the existence of a trade-off between inflation and unemployment is known as the Phillips Curve. The *evidence* was challenged vigorously by the monetary policy advocates, and later, it was refuted with the advent of the rational expectation hypothesis. To fully understand the details of these issues, the reader should consult books on both fiscal and monetary policy.

A book about money and financial systems, such as this one, should be used to gain knowledge about the role of money in the economy and as the foundation for understanding what could happen when money is added or taken from the economy. The government intervenes in the economy through both fiscal and monetary policies. This book provides the necessary foundation to be able to comprehend books covering these topics.

Notes

Chapter 1

1. Naghshpour (2013b).
2. Naghshpour (2013a).
3. Fisher (1911).
4. Naghshpour (2012c).
5. Teigen (1964).
6. Sims (1972).
7. Hume (1748).
8. Friedman (1956).

Chapter 2

1. Federal Reserve Statistical Release (2013a).
2. Federal Reserve Statistical Release (2013b).
3. Baumol (1952).
4. Tobin (1956).
5. Keynes (1936).
6. Baumol (1977).
7. Naghshpour (2012a).

Chapter 3

1. Keynes (1936).

Chapter 4

1. Friedman (1956).
2. Patinkin (1969).
3. Naghshpour (2012a).
4. Naghshpour (2012b).

Chapter 5

1. Federal Reserve System (2005).
2. Naghshpour (2013a).

3. Federal Reserve Board (2005).
4. Laeven and Valencia (2010).
5. Laeven and Valencia (2012).
6. Johnson (2010).

Chapter 6

1. Bernanke (2006).
2. Anderson and Kavajecz (1994).
3. Friedman and Heller (1969).
4. Gilbert, R. A. (1986).

Chapter 9

1. Naghshpour (2012a).
2. Markowitz (1952).
3. Neumann and Oskar (2007).
4. Nash (1950).
5. Nash (1951).
6. Cournot (1838).

Chapter 10

1. Akerlof (1970).
2. Myers and Majluf (1984).
3. Greenwald, Stiglitz and Weiss (1984).

Chapter 11

1. Keynes (1936).
2. Hicks (1937).
3. Naghshpour (2013b).
4. Carroll (2001).
5. Jappelli and Pistaferri (2009).

Chapter 12

1. Naghshpour (2013a).

Glossary

Adverse Selection: occurs when a borrower who has no intention of paying back the loan would not divulge his intention.

Assets: are the collection of valuable goods and financial documents that can be exchanged for money.

Asymmetry of Information: exists when one party in a transaction has more information about the risk and other characteristics of the transaction than does the other party.

Auction Markets: are financial markets where the price is determined by the biddings of buyers and sellers.

Bankers' Acceptance Notes: are financial instruments created by banks to facilitate transactions between international borrowers and lenders.

Barter: is the exchange of one thing for another, when neither is "money."

Benchmark Interest Rate: is the lowest interest rate for the most favorable borrower.

Break-Even Point: is the point where the cost and revenue of an investment are equal. A firm operates beyond its break-even point.

Capital: refers to *real* assets such as factories, raw materials, machinery, and inventory of goods, either in the process of production or finished.

Capital Budgeting: is an investment decision process that is used to determine the profitability of investments.

Capital Markets: are financial markets where intermediate- and long-term debt instruments are exchanged.

Commercial Papers: are issued by well-known firms and financial institutions to raise funds.

Consumer Advisory Council: is part of the Federal Reserve System and focuses on the Board's responsibilities outlined in the Consumer Credit Protection Act.

Convertible Bonds: are corporate financial papers that can be converted to equity at a given rate of conversion.

Corporate Bonds: are intermediate- to long-term instruments issued by large and reputable corporations to raise capital.

Debt: is any fund borrowed for new investment.

Demand Deposit: is a checking account.

Demand for Money for Transaction: is the portion of demand for money needed for transactions.

Derivative Markets: are financial markets in which the settlement of a financial transaction occurs at a time later than the time of transaction.

Direct Finance: is when the lender buys shares of a company directly without intervention from a financial intermediary.

Discount Factor: is the ratio used to convert future revenue to its present value equivalent. It is equal to the inverse of (1 + the interest rate).

Discount Rate: is the interest rate used in the discount factor to obtain the present value of future revenue. It is the opportunity cost of receiving your money in the future instead of now.

Discounted Present Value: converts streams of future earnings into their value at the present time.

Dividend: is the payment of a firm's profit to those with an equity share.

Edge Act: refers to the 1919 amendment to the Federal Reserve Act of 1913. It allows the national banks to conduct international transactions through federally charted subsidiaries.

Equation of Exchange: is the name of the formula that represents the classic quantity theory.

Equity Share: is the portion of a company that belongs to the shareholder. It entitles the holder to a share of a company's profit. The equity owner shares the business risk.

Eurodollars: are U.S. dollars that are in banks outside of the U.S.

Exchanges: are auction markets.

The **Federal Advisory Council:** is part of the Federal Reserve and provides advice and consultation on all matters within the Board's jurisdiction.

Federal Fund: is an overnight loan that banks deposit with the Federal Reserve banks.

Federal Funds Rate: is the interest rate charged on federal funds overnight loans.

Federal Open Market Committee: is the part of Federal Reserve responsible for regulating the supply of money created by the banking system.

Financial Futures: is a financial market, in which the entire transaction is finalized at a set time in the future, the price of which will be determined at the time of settlement.

Financial Innovations: are the same thing as a financial product or service.

Financial Instruments: are the means through which financial intermediaries facilitate transactions.

Financial Intermediaries: are institutions that facilitate monetary transactions by collecting loanable funds from savers and disbursing it among the borrowers at market clearing interest rates, adjusted for risk and uncertainty.

Financial Markets: represent the physical and virtual locations where financial transactions take place.

Fiscal Policy: is the collection of decisions on how to spend government expenditures to influence the course of the economy.

Inflation: is an increase in the overall price level.

Information Asymmetry: exists when one party of the transaction has more information about the pertinent factors than the other party.

Interest Rate: is the price of lending and borrowing money.

Internal Rate of Return: is the rate used to discount the flow of anticipated future revenues of an investment in capital budgeting.

Investment: is the production or acquisition of new real capital assets.

IS Curve: is the loci of interest rate–output sets for which the goods market is in equilibrium.

Liquidity: of money refers to the ease of spending it.

LM schedule: is the loci of interest rates and incomes that result in equilibrium in the money market.

M1: definition of money consists of (1) currency outside the U.S. Treasury, Federal Reserve banks, and the vaults of depository institutions; (2) traveler's checks of nonbank issuers; (3) demand deposits at commercial bａnks (excluding those amounts held by depository institutions, the U.S. government, and foreign banks and official institutions) less cash items in the process of collection and Federal Reserve float; and (4) other checkable deposits (OCDs), consisting of negotiable order of withdrawal (NOW) and automatic transfer service (ATS) accounts at depository institutions, credit union share draft accounts, and demand deposits at thrift institutions.

M2: definition of money consists of M1 plus (1) savings deposits (including money market deposit accounts); (2) small-denomination time deposits (time deposits in amounts of less than $100,000), less individual retirement account (IRA) and Keogh balances at depository institutions; and (3) balances in retail money market mutual funds, less IRA and Keogh balances at money market mutual funds.

M3: definition of money consists of M2 plus time deposits at mutual savings banks and savings and loan associations, and shares held at credit unions.

M4: definition of money consists of M2 plus negotiable CDs over $100,000.

M5: definition of money consists of M3 plus negotiable CDs over $100,000.

Marginal Cost: is the cost of producing an additional unit of a good.

Marginal Efficiency of Investment: is another name for internal rate of return.

Marginal Propensity to Consume: represents the change in consumption due to one unit change in income. It is equal to 1-MPS.

Marginal Propensity to Save: represents the change in savings due to one unit change in income. It is equal to 1-MPC.

Marginal Utility: is the utility of consuming an additional unit.

Money: is anything that is customarily accepted by parties in exchange of a good, a service, or a financial arrangement.

Money Markets: are where short-term debt instruments are exchanged.

Money Market Instruments: are securities and investments by private enterprises.

Moral Hazard: occurs when the action of one party has a detrimental effect on the other party of a transaction.

Multiplier Effect: is the sum of all the increases in income due to repeated cycles of income–consumption generated by an initial increase in income. It is equal to the inverse of marginal propensity to save times the magnitude of change in income.

Negotiable Bank Certificates of Deposits (CD): is a fixed maturity instrument with a higher interest rate than savings accounts.

Net Interest Margin: refers to the difference in borrowing and lending interest rates charged by commercial bands.

Nominal Interest Rate: is the prevailing market interest rate.

Nominal Value: is any economic value that is not adjusted for inflation.

Option: is when the price of a transaction is left to be decided in the future at the time the goods change hand.

Overnight Rate: is the interest that is charged when banks borrow from one another or the Federal Reserve Bank.

Over-the-Counter Exchanges: are stock exchanges that do not have a central location.

The Paradox of Thrift: refers to the fact that an increase in the marginal propensity to save causes a smaller multiplier effect and thus smaller national income.

Permanent Income: is the expected long-run income.

Portfolio Motive: is the demand for money to obtain stocks and other assets that provide earnings.

Price of Money: is the return to lending money; it is the same as the interest.

Primary Markets: are the type of market where a newly issued claim is sold to an initial buyer.

Profit (economic): is the excess of revenue after all resources are paid. It is less than the accounting profit, which includes the return to capital. Under a perfectly competitive market, the economic profit is zero.

Quantity Theory of Money: is the expression that the value of money in circulation is equal to the value of all transactions in the country in one year.

Real Value: is any economic variable that is adjusted for inflation by dividing its nominal value by the inflation rate.

Recession: is a decrease in overall production.

Repurchase Agreements: are used by large corporations for cash management for a very short term, up to a maximum of two weeks.

Required Reserve: is the minimum amount of cash on hand at the end of each business day that commercial banks must hold. The percentage of cash holdings to total amount of assets of the bank is determined by the Federal Reserve. Controlling the reserve controls the amount of money banks can create.

Risk-Averse: is anyone who dislikes risk, other things equal.

Risk-Earnings Possibility Curve: represents the pairs of risk–earning where higher risks are as preferable as lower risks because of their higher earnings.

A **Savings Account:** is an interest earning bank deposit. It used to be less liquid than the checking account.

Secondary Financial Markets: are markets in which existing financial papers are traded.

State and Local Government Bonds: (municipal bonds) are intermediate- to long-term bonds, but are issued by municipalities and state governments.

Standard Deviation: is the square root of variance and represents the average error of a variable. It is a measure of risk of financial transactions.

Stocks: are equities of corporations that are traded in the stock exchange. Their value determines the asset values of the issuing firm.

The **Thrift Institutions Advisory Council:** is part of the Federal Reserve and is charged with oversight of the thrift institutions and the Depository Institution Deregulation and Monetary Control Act.

A **Time Deposit:** is a savings account.

Transaction Demand: is the portion of money demanded to purchase goods and services.

Transaction Theory: is a theory that explains part of the demand for money used for transactions only.

Transitory Income: is any income that is not expected to occur regularly.

U.S. Government Agency Securities: are intermediate- to long-term bonds; government-sponsored agencies, as well as the federal government, can issue them.

U.S. Treasury Bills: (T-bills) are the most liquid financial instruments. They are issued by the U.S. government and are short-term debt obligations.

U.S. Treasury Securities: are intermediate- to long-term bonds issued by the federal government.

Variance: is the sum of the squares of the deviations of values from their mean, divided by population size. It is the average of the squared individual errors.

Velocity: of money represents the average number of times money changes hand in a year.

References

Akerlof, G. (1970). The market for 'lemons': Quality, uncertainty and the market mechanism. *Quarterly Journal of Economics 84*(3), 488–500.

Anderson, R. G., & Kavajecz, K. (1994). A historical perspective on the Federal reserve's monetary aggregates: Definition, construction, and targeting. *Federal Reserve Bank of St. Louis Review 76*(2), 1–66.

Baumol, W. J. (1952). The transactions demand for cash: An inventory theoretic approach. *Quarterly Journal of Economics 66*(4), 545–556.

Baumol, W. J. (1977). *Economic theory and operations analysis*. Englewood Hills, NJ: Prentice Hall.

Bernanke, B. S. "*Monetary Aggregates and Monetary Policy at the Federal Reserve: A Historical Perspective*." Presentation to Fourth FCB Central Banking Conference, November 10, 2006, Frankfurt, Germany. Available at http://www.federalreserve.gov/newsevents/speech/bernanke20061110a.htm. Accessed on March 20, 2013.

Carroll, C. D. (2001). "*Precautionary saving and the marginal propensity to consume out of permanent income*." No. w8233. National Bureau of Economic Research.

Cournot, A. A. (1838). English translation by N. T. Bacon. (1927). *Researchers into the mathematical principles of the theory of wealth (Recherches sur les principes mathematiques de la theorie de richesses)*. New York: Macmillan & Co.

Federal Reserve Board. (2005). *The twelve federal reserve districts*. Last updated December 13, 2005, from http://www.federalreserve.gov/otherfrb.htm. Accessed on March 20, 2013.

Federal Reserve Statistical Release. (2013a). Released on January 16, 2013, from http://www.federalreserve.gov/releases/g17/Current/default.htm. Accessed on March 20, 2013.

Federal Reserve Statistical Release. (2013b). Released on January 31, 2013, from http://www.federalreserve.gov/releases/h6/current/h6.htm. Accessed on March 20, 2013.

Federal Reserve System. (2005). *The Federal Reserve System: Purposes and functions* (9th ed.). Washington DC: Board of Governors of the Federal Reserve System, from http://www.federalreserve.gov/pf/pdf/pf_complete.pdf. Accessed on March 20, 2013.

Fisher, I. (1911). *The purchasing power of money, its determination and relation to credit, interest, and crises*. New York: The Macmillan Company.

Friedman, M. (1956). "The quantity theory of money—a restatement." In M. Friedman (Ed.), *Studies in the quantity theory of money* (pp. 3–21). Chicago, IL: University of Chicago Press.

Friedman, M., & Heller W. H. (1969). *Monetary vs. fiscal policy*. New York: W.W. Norton & Company, Inc.

Gilbert, R. A. Requiem for Regulation Q: What It Did and Why It Passed Away. Federal Reserve Bank of St. Louis, February 1986, Available at *http://www.research.stlouisfed.org/publications/review/86/.../Requiem_Feb1986.pdf.* Accessed on March 20, 2013.

Greenwald, B., Stiglitz, J. E., & Weiss, A. (1984). Information imperfections in the capital market and macroeconomic fluctuations. *The American Economic Review 74*(2), 194–199.

Hicks, J. R. (1937). Mr. Keynes and the classics: A suggested interpretation. *Econometrica 5*(2), 147–159.

Hume, D. (1748). *Essays, moral, political, and literary,* from http://files.libertyfund.org/files/704/Hume_0059.pdf#page=4. Accessed on March 20, 2013.

Jappelli, T., & Pistaferri, L. (2009). *The consumption response to income changes* (Discussion Paper No. 08-52). Stanford Institute for Economic Policy Research.

Johnson, R. T. (2010). *Historical beginnings ... The Federal Reserve System*. Boston, MA: Federal Reserve Bank of Boston.

Keynes, J. M. (1936) [2006]. *The general theory of employment, interest and money*. Delhi, India: Atlantic Publishers and Distributors.

Laeven, L., & Valencia, F. (2010). *Resolution of banking crises: The good, the bad, and the ugly.* IMF Working Paper 10/146. Washington, DC: International Monetary Fund.

Laeven, L., & Valencia, F. (2012). Systematic banking crises database: An update. IMF Working Paper 12/163. Washington, DC: International Monetary Fund.

Keynes, John Maynard. 1936 [2006]. *The General Theory of Employment, Interest and Money*. Dehli, India: Atlantic Publishers and Distributors.

Markowitz, H. (1952). Portfolio selection. *The Journal of Finance 7*(1), 77–91.

Myers, S. C., & Majluf, N. S. (1984). Corporate financing and investment decisions when firms have information that investors do not have. *Journal of Financial Economics 13*, 187–221.

Naghshpour, S. (2012a). *Statistics for economics*. New York: Business Expert Press.

Naghshpour, S. (2012b). *Regression for economics*. New York: Business Expert Press.

Naghshpour, S. (2012c). "Monetary Theory and the struggle with discretion versus rule-based policy". In M. Majumdar (Ed.), *Fundamental economics (Encyclopedia of Life Support Systems)*, UNESCO. Oxford: Eolss Publishers.

Naghshpour, S. (2013a). *Monetary policy*. New York: Business Expert Press.

Naghshpour, S. (2013b). *Fiscal policy*. New York: Business Expert Press.

Nash, J. (1950). Equilibrium points in n-person games. *Proceedings of the National Academy of Sciences 36*(1), 48–49.

Nash, J. (1951). Non-cooperative games. *The Annals of Mathematics 54*(2), 286–295.

Patinkin, D. (1969). The Chicago tradition, the quantity theory, and Friedman. *Journal of Money, Credit and Banking 1*(1), 46–70.

Patinkin , D. (1986). Money and wealth: A review article. *Journal of Economic Literature 7*(4), 1140–1160.

Sims, C. A. (1972). Money, income, and causality. *The American Economic Review 62*(4), 540–552.

Teigen, R. L. (1964). Demand and supply functions for money in the United States structural estimates. *Econometrica 32*(4), 476–509.

Tobin, J. (1956). The interest elasticity of the transactions demand for cash. *Review of Economics and Statistics 38*(3), 241–247.

von Neumann, J., & Oskar, M. (2007). *Theory of games and economic behavior*. (60th Anniversary ed.). Princeton, NJ: Princeton University Press.

Index

OTHER TITLES IN OUR ECONOMICS COLLECTION

Philip Romero, The University of Oregon and Jeffrey Edwards,
North Carolina A&T State University, Collection Editors

- *Managerial Economics: Concepts and Principles* by Donald N. Stengel
- *Your Macroeconomic Edge: Investing Strategies for the Post-Recession World* by Philip J. Romero
- *Working with Economic Indicators: Interpretation and Sources* by Donald N. Stengel and Priscilla Chaffe-Stengel
- *Innovative Pricing Strategies to Increase Profits* by Daniel Marburger
- *Regression for Economics* by Shahdad Naghshpour
- *Statistics for Economics* by Shahdad Naghshpour
- *How Strong Is Your Firm's Competitive Advantage?* by Daniel Marburger
- *A Primer on Microeconomics* by Thomas Beveridge
- *Game Theory: Anticipating Reactions for Winning Actions* by Mark L. Burkey
- *A Primer on Macroeconomics* by Thomas Beveridge
- *International Economics: Understanding the Forces of Globalization for Managers* by Paul Torelli
- *Recovering from the Global Financial Crisis: Achieving Financial Stability in Times of Uncertainty* by Marianne Ojo

Announcing the Business Expert Press Digital Library

*Concise E-books Business Students Need for Classroom
and Research*

This book can also be purchased in an e-book collection by your library as
- a one-time purchase,
- that is owned forever,
- allows for simultaneous readers,
- has no restrictions on printing, and
- can be downloaded as PDFs from within the library community.

Our digital library collections are a great solution to beat the rising cost of textbooks. e-books can be loaded into their course management systems or onto student's e-book readers.

The **Business Expert Press** digital libraries are very affordable, with no obligation to buy in future years. For more information, please visit **www.businessexpertpress.com/librarians**. To set up a trial in the United States, please contact **Adam Chesler** at *adam.chesler@ businessexpertpress.com* for all other regions, contact **Nicole Lee** at *nicole.lee@igroupnet.com*.

0 1341 1571076 3

CPSIA information can be obtained at www.ICGtesting.com
Printed in the USA
LVOW07s2225101213

364793LV00014B/385/P

9 781606 494844